PRAISE FOR *SHAMELESS*

Marilyn provides a rare insider's view of the power of political change and proves with *Shameless* that she is as fearless as a writer as she was as a politician.

—Olivia Chow, former Toronto City Councillor and MP Trinity-Spadina

Shameless is a fantastic book. Marilyn's story reflects a similar journey that both myself and my birth mother, Joni Mitchell, experienced and the joy we felt when we reunited. Secrecy was so entrenched that it took years just to get a piece of paper that didn't even have her name on it. Because of the changes in adoption disclosure laws, people can now get the information they need to search. Thanks Marilyn!

—Kilauren Gibb (Little Green), adoptee and artist

Marilyn Churley has skilfully interwoven personal and political narratives detailing the struggle to know one's history and kin. Through her courageous determination, she has made a lasting contribution to opening adoption records. This book stands as a testament to what a principled politician can accomplish.

—Michael Grand, professor of clinical psychology, University of Guelph and author of *The Adoption Constellation*

Shameless will counter stereotypes and reverse the undeserved shame suffered by the many millions of us who experienced the tragic non-choice of surrendering our babies to adoption. We are ordinary women—teachers, administrators, lawyers, healthcare workers, and politicians—trapped in extraordinary circumstances. Coming forward in the Ontario legislature as one of us, and holding the standard of open records through difficult years, Marilyn joined with the grassroots in wrenching adoption out of shadowy decades of damaging secrecy. This is a story that needs to be shared in schools of social work, halls of medicine, and pulpits everywhere.

    —Karen Lynn, President, Canadian Council of Natural Mothers

The million-plus members of Ontario's adoption community owe a debt of thanks to Marilyn Churley. Without her integrity, and her willingness to stand up and be counted among us, we might still be waiting for access to our own records. *Shameless* is Churley's modest account of the impact her reunion and her advocacy in the Ontario Legislature played in redressing the wrongs imposed by sealed records.

    —Holly Kramer, past president of Parent Finders Incorporated

While the decade-plus-long struggle for adoption disclosure law reform had personal meaning for Marilyn, her passionate and tireless efforts were driven by her fierce commitment to justice and equality and her desire to give voice to those who needed an advocate inside the chambers of power. *Shameless* documents the personal and the political and how, when they come together, change gets made.

    —Hon. Frances Lankin, former MPP Beaches-East York

I wept. I didn't expect to, but I wept. I wept for Marilyn's humiliations, her loss, her joy of reuniting with her son, her determination, her dogged determination to change the system, her passion and compassion. I wept because with honesty and candor Marilyn took me with her: "unwed" mom, birth mother, alone again, married woman, mom again, elected politician. She took me with her to places I had never been. Perhaps you have been there yourself and it will be familiar. If not, you will experience the complexities, the surprising brutality, the love, the hope of young moms longing for their own. As a politician Marilyn gets it right! The marriage of compassion and justice, real social justice influencing policy. Read this book and believe it is possible.

—Gerry Rogers MHA St. John's Centre, feminist filmmaker

Never did a Bill signed into law hold such emotion for so many! That was the adoption law that finally made its way through the Ontario legislature. Marilyn may have been on the other side of the House, but she worked with me to open adoption records, all partisanship aside. The chronicling of her life through *Shameless* is inspiring. It's clear the new law was the moment for Marilyn to exhale, and for the adoption community to cheer.

—Sandra Pupatello, former Minister of
Community and Social Services

MARILYN CHURLEY

SHAMELESS

THE FIGHT
FOR ADOPTION DISCLOSURE
AND THE SEARCH
FOR MY SON

Between the Lines | *Toronto, Canada*

Shameless

First published in 2015 by
Between the Lines
401 Richmond Street West, Studio 277
Toronto, Ontario M5V 3A8 Canada
1-800-718-7201
www.btlbooks.com

LIBRARY AND ARCHIVES CANADA CATALOGUING IN PUBLICATION

Churley, Marilyn, author
Shameless : the fight for adoption disclosure and the search for my son / Marilyn Churley.

Includes index.
Issued in print and electronic formats.
ISBN 978-1-77113-173-5 (pbk.).—ISBN 978-1-77113-174-2 (epub).—ISBN 978-1-77113-175-9 (pdf)

1. Churley, Marilyn. 2. Mothers and sons—Ontario—Biography.
3. Politicians—Ontario—Biography. 4. Adopted children—Ontario—
Biography. 5. Adoption—Law and legislation—Ontario.
6. Disclosure of information—Law and legislation—Ontario. I. Title.

HV875.58.C3205 2015   362.73409713   C2014-906713-5   C2014-906714-3

Text and cover design by Ingrid Paulson
Printed in Canada

Between the Lines gratefully acknowledges assistance for its publishing activities from the Canada Council for the Arts, the Ontario Arts Council, the Government of Ontario through the Ontario Book Publishers Tax Credit program and through the Ontario Book Initiative, and the Government of Canada through the Canada Book Fund.

Canada Council Conseil des arts
for the Arts   du Canada

Canadä

ONTARIO ARTS COUNCIL
CONSEIL DES ARTS DE L'ONTARIO
An Ontario government agency
un organisme du gouvernement de l'Ontario

This book is dedicated to my beloved children, Astra and Billy

You're sad and you're sorry but you're not ashamed
—Joni Mitchell, "Little Green" from *Blue*, 1971

CONTENTS

PREFACE

BEGAN WORKING ON updating Ontario's adoption disclosure laws in the mid-1990s as a member of provincial parliament (MPP). Many people who worked with me over the years urged me to write a book about how we were able to get new laws passed. However, I must stress that this is not meant to be a definitive account. This is a memoir based on my personal and political experience. It's also a story of losing and finding, pain and joy, and how to fight and win against powerful forces.

I met and worked with a lot of wonderful people from the adoption community throughout the years. Naturally I focus on those with whom I worked most closely, but I want to thank everyone who worked on this issue and who came before us. Your commitment to the cause provided the foundation that we built on.

I have strived to be accurate and honest while telling my story, but, of course, memory can sometimes play funny tricks on us. I went back and consulted old letters and papers to help me with some of the personal details. For committee hearing testimony and statements made in the legislature, I drew on the Debates and Proceedings of the Legislative Assembly of Ontario (Hansard). Where, to avoid causing pain or harm, I have taken the liberty of changing some names, that is indicated in the text.

ACKNOWLEDGEMENTS

It took many years to write this book. It would not have been possible without the support and help of many people.

A great big thank you to my friends Holly Kramer, Karen Lynn, Wendy Rowney, Pat McDermott, Sarah Jordison, Lesley Mang, and Coleman Romalis for reading the manuscript and for your excellent advice. You all dazzle me with your intelligence, kindness, and sense of humour.

Thanks to my friend, award-winning documentary filmmaker Liam Romalis, and Jason Charters, Mako Funasaka, and Enza Apa of Riddle Films for the superb trailer they made for the book. You guys are so talented!

I was lucky to find former *Toronto Star* and now freelance editor Hope Kamin through my friend Ian Urquhart. She took on a mountain of material and cut it down to a manageable and readable manuscript and made sense of things that initially did not make any sense at all. Thank you, Hope.

Thank you to the team at Between the Lines for reviewing the manuscript and making critical suggestions that greatly improved it. You guys are the best! I also want to thank Between the Lines for assigning freelance editor Tilman Lewis to help polish the manuscript before publication. It was important to me to work with an editor who "got" me. He did fabulous work without diminishing my voice. Thanks, Tilman.

I want to acknowledge my brothers and sisters, Edna, Max, Joan, and Fred, for checking family facts from time to time. All of my siblings are attractive, smart, and funny and they can write better than I can. Edna, I stole some of your words when describing Mom and Dad because they are so good.

Thanks to the good people of Restoule, where my cottage is located and where I started and finished this book. In particular I want to thank my neighbours Bob and Katy Laplante and friends Frances Lankin and Wayne Campbell, who dragged me away from my desk and took me to fish fries and the Legion when I needed a break.

I want to thank my husband, Richard Barry, who gave me excellent writing advice and put up with a lot of moaning and groaning as I struggled to find the time and energy to write between running in two federal elections, family obligations, and working a full-time job. Richard, your support and confidence saw me through and out the other side of those hard moments when I just wanted to give up.

And finally, heartfelt thanks and endless love go to my *two* children, Astra and Billy, for their encouragement and love. They and my grandsons, James and Tristan, are shining jewels that make my life rich and wonderful.

A NOTE ON LANGUAGE

Adoption in Canada is defined as "the legal transfer of parental rights and obligations from birth parent(s) to adoptive parent(s)."

In the legal language used in most jurisdictions, biological mothers are referred to as "birth mothers." However, the language surrounding adoption has evolved over the years and many mothers have come to regard this term as derogatory, as relegating them to being simply "breeders" or "former" mothers of their children. Many women prefer the term "natural" or "first" mother, but some adoptive parents feel that term implies that there is something "unnatural" about them as parents or that they come "second" as parents.

I have found it impossible to find language that everyone in the adoption triangle can support. In the end, for clarity and consistency, I've opted to use the legal terms "birth mother" and "birth parents."

INTRODUCTION

O N JANUARY 30, 1968, at the age of nineteen, I delivered a seven-pound, thirteen-ounce boy in a hospital in Barrie, Ontario. I named him Andrew Fitz-Patrick. I never got to hold him. I signed him away—out of my life—to strangers. There were no supports for single moms, and many women at the time would rather have died than find themselves pregnant out of wedlock.

This is not an unusual story. It is far more common than most people are aware. In her 2006 book *The Girls Who Went Away*, American writer Ann Fessler states that in the United States in the decades between the Second World War and *Roe v. Wade*, 1.5 million young women were secretly sent to homes for unwed mothers and coerced into giving their babies up for adoption.

In kindly Canada, many thousands of young women suffered the same fate in that same time period. If you combine the number of women who gave away their babies with the numbers of adoptees, biological fathers, adoptive parents, siblings, grandparents, and other relatives from all sides, several million people in Canada and the United States are connected to this issue. The story is made more painful by the imposed secrecy, the shame, and the denial of human rights.

The movie *Philomena* tells the moving story of one unwed, pregnant Irish girl who was sent off to a "Magdalene Laundry," a business run by Irish nuns. They forced unmarried pregnant girls, as well as women who were considered too pretty, tempting to men, mentally disabled, or strong-willed into asylums, where in addition to other abuse, their babies would be taken from them. Philomena's child was allowed to stay in the home with her for three years, then was taken away and given up for adoption to a couple from the United States.

Of course, women have been having children out of wedlock since the beginning of time. Some pregnancies were brought under an umbrella of respectability by shotgun marriages. Other young women had no choice but to bear the shame of having the child in their own communities and sometimes allowing their parents to raise the child as their own. Some attempted to self-abort, often mangling themselves in the process, and others would risk backstreet abortions, which all too often would leave them gravely injured and infertile— and sometimes, kill them.

I tried to go it alone. Rather than confess my supposed sin to my parents, I kept my secret and spent the months of my pregnancy with friends.

I see what happened to me and to countless other women through a feminist perspective, a perspective that is little represented in the adoption books that I am familiar with. In these stories, a distinction is often made between the "good" pregnant girl who made a mistake and was ashamed of it and the "bad" girl who was promiscuous.

I really hate that word. It only applies to girls. Boys were just sowing their wild oats—doing what comes naturally. They were rarely blamed and shamed as the girls were. And the double standards of the mid to late 1960s were breathtaking. A sexual revolution was happening; women were fighting for equality, and being sexually active was part of that equality. Yet it was nearly impossible for unmarried women to get birth control, abortion was illegal, and despite the changes in socially accepted behaviour, the system continued to treat unmarried pregnant girls like "sluts" and even criminals.

Women have always been coerced into living their lives as society deems appropriate, and tormented, punished, and shamed when they didn't comply. And they still are: witness the phenomenon of "slut walks" that started in Toronto in 2011 after a police officer told women at a university safety forum that, in order not to be victimized, they should avoid dressing like sluts. In some parts of the world, women continue to have few human rights. At least in most of the Western world, reproductive rights have greatly improved. Women are able to access birth control and obtain safe, legal abortions. But we must not take these hard-earned rights for granted. Some doctors in Canada are refusing to prescribe birth control pills, citing religious reasons; access to abortion in New Brunswick has been greatly reduced and there continues to be no access at all in Prince Edward Island. In the United States, there have been numerous and alarming setbacks to reproductive rights for women and families.

I know there are people who will say that it is wrong of me to support abortion because if I had terminated my pregnancy, the son whom I love so much would not have been born. That fact is indisputable. But in initially seeking out an abortion, I attempted to do a reasonable thing given my situation at the time. I believe we are all here by chance—if my father hadn't tripped over my mother's feet in a friend's kitchen, I wouldn't exist. As things turned out, my son is here and I am very glad he is. But a woman's right to choose and have control over her own body is a fundamental human right that I strongly support.

Much has been written about the pain, the humiliation, the wrenching loneliness and monumental loss that a mother experiences when giving up her newborn for adoption. I didn't forget my baby; mothers don't forget their babies. Instead, I was sentenced to years of grief, longing, and rage.

But more than twenty years after relinquishing my child at birth, I landed in a position of power, with the ability to change adoption disclosure laws to help adoptees and birth parents find each other. Elected as an MPP in the September 1990 election that, against all odds, brought the New Democratic Party to power in Ontario, I became minister of consumer and commercial relations and the registrar general of Ontario. Suddenly, I was in charge of every birth record in the province! My son's birth records, locked away in files in Thunder Bay, were under my watch. I still didn't know where he was, what he looked like, what talents he might have. Was he a musician like his birth father? Was he a good debater and politically active like me? I didn't even know whether he was alive.

I eventually found my son through private means, but at the same time, I carried on the long struggle to reform laws to make birth records available to adult adoptees and their birth parents in Ontario. There were many obstacles, and, over more than a decade, a number of failed attempts to have legislation passed. Things finally came together on October 31, 2005, and I wept at what seemed like reaching the finish line after a marathon.

Many people were part of my journey—from the family I first left in Labrador in 1966 to my daughter, who was born in 1974; to my son, whom I found in 1996; to the remarkable birth parents, adoptees, and adoptive parents who worked with me over the years; to my political colleagues, who included the late NDP leader Jack Layton, former Ontario premiers Bob Rae, Mike Harris, Ernie Eves, and Dalton McGuinty, and Premier Kathleen Wynne.

By the time we succeeded in reforming Ontario's adoption disclosure laws, my son was very much present in my life. It was a long and difficult battle, but I never once felt like giving up. Some people said I was trying to change the laws so everyone could have the same outcome I'd had—a happy reunion. That would be nice if it were possible, but it wasn't my goal. I simply wanted equality for adoptees, so that they could have access to their own personal birth information just like everyone else. And I wanted biological mothers to be given the right to find out what had happened to their children. It will always be up to the parties to decide if they want to meet or have a relationship.

Losing a child is almost unbearable. It leaves a lasting mark. But human beings can also heal and find ways to overcome tragedy. Although I express a great deal of pain and anger in this book, there is also an abundance of joy. Finding my son gave me peace of mind; ironically, it freed me from having to worry about him every day. From the moment of our reunion, I knew he was alive and well. I knew who he was, and now, I know where he is. I know we will be getting together for dinner soon.

I can tell the world I have not one, but two children—something I couldn't do for a long time. I wasn't there when my son blew out his first birthday candle, but I was filled with joy to be present to celebrate the birthday of his little boy, my grandson. My broken family had been knitted back together.

PART I

GOODBYE, LITTLE BABY

ONE

A CALL FROM THE PREMIER

O N A SUNNY MORNING in the fall of 1993 I sat in my downtown Toronto office, drinking a cup of coffee and reading the morning headlines. As I enjoyed the spectacular view of Lake Ontario, I scanned some background notes my staff had put together about the funeral services sector. In half an hour, I'd meet representatives from funeral homes and cemeteries who wanted legislative changes, and they were feuding.

I scolded myself, and chuckled at the same time, about some awful puns I'd blurted out during my last early-morning meeting with these people—there will be stiff opposition to this; I understand you have grave concerns. Just then my executive assistant, Karen Todkill, rushed in. "The premier is on the phone for you," she announced.

"Why would he call me at this hour of the morning?" I said, thinking, *Why he is calling me at all? I must be in trouble.*

"Minister, I need your help," Bob Rae said when I picked up the phone. Groups representing adoptees and birth parents were lobbying hard for our government to reform Ontario's adoption disclosure laws. He told me that the issue had been discussed at the last cabinet meeting, which I had missed, and that my support as registrar general of Ontario would be instrumental.

My heart skipped a beat. I did not want to get involved with this. But as registrar general, I had no choice.

That was how it all began.

In the early 1990s, members of the Toronto and Ottawa chapters of Parent Finders and the Adoption Council of Ontario met for many months on Saturday mornings and sometimes weeknights. A lawyer, Corinne Robertshaw, was helping them pro bono to write a brief to the newly minted minister of community and social services, Tony Silipo. During this exercise, the quest for adoption disclosure reform was identified as a human rights issue. The adoption community felt that framing the issue this way was a huge step forward for the movement. Now they could to begin to demand equal rights with non-adopted adults born in Ontario.

Parent Finders, the Adoption Council of Ontario, and other activists representing adoptees, birth parents, and adoptive parents from across the province lobbied for action on promises the government had made to reform adoption disclosure laws. They wanted previously sealed records to be released to adult adoptees so that they could learn about their original identity, ethnicity, and medical history. They submitted briefs and protested on the lawns of Queen's Park. (Those lawns in front of the legislature saw considerable action at the time—our government drew a lot of protesters.)

When Rae called me, the government had still not put the adoption disclosure issue on its crowded legislative timetable. But, with the premier determined to take action, cabinet asked backbench Sault Ste. Marie MPP Tony Martin, the parliamentary assistant to the minister of community and social services, to introduce adoption disclosure legislation as a private member's bill. Martin contacted people in the adoption community who had been working on disclosure reform for many years. Together they drafted a bill that would grant adult adoptees access to their own original birth certificates, and allow birth parents who didn't want their children to contact them once they had found their information to lodge a contact veto.

Private members' bills are debated in one-hour slots one day a week when the provincial legislature is in session. Generally, private members' bills that get passed are of little substance—like a law to recognize Tartan Day in Ontario. However, because the adoption bill had the support of the premier and his cabinet, it was being processed behind the scenes as though it were a government bill. The community and social services minister and I got very involved in drafting it.

After consultation across the province, Bill 158 was introduced in the legislature in May 1994. It was, to my surprise, a controversial issue. Many Liberal and Progressive Conservative members opposed the changes and fought against the retroactivity of the bill. The debate became quite frustrating, especially as opponents used procedural tricks to keep the bill from moving forward.

It took until November for the bill to be sent to the Social Policy Committee for further study and, for what would be the seventh time since 1975, public hearings were held on adoption disclosure in Ontario. The bill was given a rocky ride by some members of the opposition parties, but eventually it was voted on and sent back to the house for further debate and a vote. There it languished; it was not back on the agenda for third reading and a final vote until the last day the legislature was to sit before an election call.

December 8, 1994, was supposed to be a momentous day for the adoption community. It was, to say the least, an emotional night for me. But few people in the legislature knew that I had a personal interest in this matter, so I tried to keep those emotions in check. The visitors' galleries were packed with ecstatic people from the adoption community who were confident that after years of work, this bill was going to pass.

What could go wrong? The government had a majority, and several members of the opposition were also expected to vote in favour. Further, an agreement had been made between the house leaders of all three parties that the bill would be debated for one hour, and the final vote would take place well before the legislature prorogued at midnight.

But not so fast. Progressive Conservatives David Tilson and Norm Sterling, Liberal Jim Bradley (who, I am pleased to say, would later change his mind and support reform), and other intransigent opponents of adoption disclosure had a plan. Breaking the all-party deal, they filibustered until the clock ran out at midnight. The vote never took place.

That they strongly opposed the bill and would vote against it was not in question. They had spoken about the need to protect aging birth mothers from being accosted at their doors by their now adult children, and about protecting adoptive parents from these birth mothers coming into their children's lives. Some of those opposed even suggested that unwed mothers who gave up their children did not deserve to have any contact with them. Still, I was shocked by their extreme emotional responses to the concept of opening records to adult adoptees. Something was going on, which would become apparent to me as the debate raged on for another decade. However, despite their strong opposition, I was shocked by their behaviour. Breaking an agreement between the house leaders was just not done.

They did it, though. As it became clear that they were going to talk the clock out and that their party leaders were going to let them, I sat there in shock.

With the clock approaching midnight, the filibuster continued. At midnight, the Speaker rose to announce that the house was adjourned. It was over.

I looked at the stricken faces in the gallery and watched Tony Martin, himself looking shocked and crestfallen, bring the visitors into the government lobby. Many were crying openly. I put my head on my desk and wept. And that was that—for the time being.

TWO

BEGINNINGS

EDDIE CHURLEY WAS twenty years old in 1945 when he met eighteen-year-old Myrtis Emberley. He went to a friend's home in Old Perlican, a little fishing outport in Trinity Bay, Newfoundland, while Myrtis happened to be visiting from her home town of Bay de Verde, the northernmost community in Conception Bay. The way my father always told the story, he saw Myrtis sitting on the corner of the day bed in the kitchen of his friend's house and tripped over her feet as he came around the corner. He was completely taken with her beauty. He often told us children that he was knocked off his feet in more ways than one. "Your mother," he'd say, "was like a little doll. She was the most beautiful girl I had ever seen." Myrtis was petite and vivacious, with a perfect oval face and big brown eyes, her glossy black hair set off by clear ivory skin. Eddie was five foot eleven, a slender, serious man with striking blue eyes and a wide, expressive mouth. Of course, to me they were simply my parents, but I've seen pictures and I can verify that my father and mother made a handsome couple.

Eddie had limited education. Like most teen boys from poor fishing families, he had dropped out of school to go out to sea with his father. But even though he left school, school never left him. He had a sharp, inquisitive mind, and eventually acquired his high school diploma and an engineering degree. Eddie had strong core values, which he strived to live by and expected others to live by as well.

My beautiful mother, Myrtis.

My mother was small in stature, but she had a generous soul, spirit, and capacity to love and to laugh. She took what life handed her in stride and didn't spend her time grasping for things she couldn't have. She'd look at a star in the night sky, a flower, or any little critter, wild or tame, and delight in the wonder of them all.

Shortly after their auspicious meeting, Eddie and Myrtis got married. Eddie returned to his job as a cook at the American air force base in Goose Bay. Myrtis, eighteen and already pregnant, was left behind in Old Perlican to live with Eddie's parents. Having left her friends in Bay de Verde, she could not have had an easy life, especially since her in-laws were, by all accounts, not happy with the turn of events. Evidently, folks in Old Perlican looked down their noses at Bay de Verders, and Myrtis was not considered good enough for Eddie. I'm happy to say that changed over the years, and my mother became much beloved by both her mother- and father-in-law.

In mid-1948, when my sister Edna was two years old and I was six weeks, my father had saved enough money to build a little log house, and he brought us to join him in Labrador. We were one of the first families to live in a newly created settlement carved out of the middle of nowhere to service the nearby American military base.

During the Second World War, the employment opportunities offered by the development of the base drew families from all over Newfoundland and Labrador. Thus, the community of Happy Valley–Goose Bay was born. The first three families to arrive to work at the construction of the base—the Saunderses, the Broomfields, and the Perraults—had come by motorboat in September 1943 from Big Bay, Davis Inlet, and Makkovik, towns on the north coast of Labrador.

Prior to the establishment of the base, what is now known as the Churchill River was called the Mishta-Shipu, or Grand River, by the trappers who used it. During the military presence, it became known as the Hamilton River, so the new village that was growing along the riverbanks was the Hamilton River Settlement. Two of my younger siblings, Max and Joan, are proud that their original birth registrations list Hamilton River Settlement as their official place of birth.

Labrador, known as the The Big Land, was described by French explorer Jacques Cartier as the land God gave to Cain. I can imagine that at first glance it looked pretty bleak, with stunted trees and little other growth. But really, it is a beautiful place that remains one of the last untamed areas in the world. When my family arrived, there were no roads in or out, and when the Hamilton River froze over, that was it for boat access until spring. Flying was the only option, but there were few commercial flights and most families couldn't afford them anyway. Local roads got us to and from the base and around "the valley" (as it was affectionately known), but, for the most part, we had to be a self-sufficient community for the winter.

Many families still used dog sleds to get around Happy Valley, North West River, and Mud Lake. We were shut out of the mainstream in many ways, yet we lived as most everyone did in North America. Mothers stayed home; fathers went to work, and when they came home, they ruled the roost. The people from both the Canadian and American air force bases looked down on the valley people, literally and figuratively.

By the time my parents moved there in the summer of 1948 (still a year before Newfoundland joined Canada), the population had grown to more than two hundred. The family moved into the log house my father had built on the banks of the Hamilton River, sur-rounded by dense woods, wildlife, and a few neighbours. The river was our backyard. It was a beautiful but treacherous expanse of water that took many lives over the years, including those of close friends of my parents. On the other side of the river were the gorgeous blue Mealy Mountains, and on clear, cold nights the northern lights streamed white, green, yellow, and red in great waves across the sky.

Max, me, Mom, and Edna playing in the snow.

The climate was subarctic—long, freezing, snowy winters with short but exquisitely warm summers. Autumn and spring usually lasted only a few weeks. Snowfall accumulated past the roofs, and there was often snow in every month except July and August. I had freckles as a child, and was told that rubbing May snow on my face would get rid of them. I got to try most every year.

We had no electricity or indoor plumbing. The house was heated with a wood stove, and the nearest store and hospital, run by the Grenfell Mission, were forty kilometres away at Northwest River. Even-tually my father installed a little generator in a shed, but until then we read and did homework by the light of oil lamps. In fact, my father got his high school diploma and his stationary engineering degree study-ing by the light of those lamps after a full shift of work. Eventually, he

worked his way up to become manager of the American air force power plant.

top: *Going to church after a big snowfall.*
bottom: *Husky dogs and an overturned sled along the frozen road.*

It was so cold at night that my mother warmed the beds before we climbed in with a flat iron that had been heated on the wood stove. Then she piled heavy army and Hudson's Bay blankets on top of us and put hot water bottles under our feet.

Most families up and down the riverbanks owned husky dogs that were tied up outside at night. It wasn't unusual to be awakened by the eerie sound of howling. Those dogs were dangerous if they got loose. More than once, returning home from the Hudson's Bay store with a bag of groceries, I was chased by wild dogs. Dropping the bags, I would run like mad for the house, and fortunately, always made it safely home. One of my friends was not so lucky. She was dragged through an opening in the sand underneath her house and badly mauled, and grew up with scars on one side of her face, a constant reminder for us to be on guard.

My father and his friends eventually built us a new house with more rooms. There were five of us children—Edna, me, Max, Joan, and baby Freddy. Edna, the eldest, was pretty, smart, and responsible. I got her hand-me-down clothes and she often helped me with my homework. I came next, but I was told that my parents really wanted a boy this time. They got their wish a mere eighteen months later when Max was born. He was cute and impish, hated school, and loved hockey. Then came Joan, who was blond and sweet and looked like a doll. Everyone adored her. She was just a little younger and always tried to keep up with us. Finally, there was little Freddy, the precious baby brother, who was precocious and funny.

Freddy contracted meningitis when he was an infant and nearly died from it. He spent most of the first three months of his life in a St. John's hospital far from home. I can't imagine what it was like for my mother not to be there for her sick baby. It must have been torture, but she really didn't have a choice but to go back to Happy Valley to care for the rest of us. Fortunately, Freddy recovered fully, and when he did come home he was spoiled by all of us.

We were forever taking in stray dogs and cats. Every dog we had was called Watch; my father had a dog named Watch as a boy and it was the only name he allowed us to use. I loved the dogs. When I was nine or ten, we had a new puppy that I had a special bond with. I would bathe him, wrap him up in a towel, and sit in the rocking chair in the basement singing him to sleep. I brought him with me

everywhere I went. Then one hot summer day as we were walking side by side, he was suddenly startled and dashed into the road, straight into the path of a truck. I saw my little dog cut

That's me, little sister Joan, Mom, and big sister Edna sitting on the "love seat" in our yard in Happy Valley.

in two by its wheels. I screamed and ran until I couldn't anymore, and finally sank down on the dusty roadside, sobbing in shock and horror. Some adults picked me up and carried me home.

After that incident, my father decided to buy a special dog to make up for the loss. He let me pick and I chose a springer spaniel, whom we named—you got it—Watch. He was a fantastic dog and I loved him, but he could not replace my dear little puppy.

I was a demure and feminine little girl in many ways, yet I envied the things my brother Max had. I particularly longed for a cowboy suit just like his, but my parents wouldn't have it. I loved dolls, but I also loved that suit—a brown suede fringed vest and matching fringed pants, a cowboy hat, and a holster that rode low on the hips with two pistols that shot real caps. Occasionally, I'd sneak off somewhere and put it on, until the day Max caught me wearing it while happily practising my draw and, outraged, he told on me.

We went to a small one-room school heated by a pot-bellied wood stove that the teachers had to stoke. Kids from all grades were crammed in together.

My first day at school did not go well. My mother dropped me off and kissed me goodbye at the door. I went in and saw children sitting in a row on a bench, with a long plank as a shared desk. The teacher tried to get me to sit right in the middle of the row of rowdy kids, but I would have none of it. It was partly that I was painfully shy. But I also desperately needed to make a trip to the outhouse and was too embarrassed to ask. I sobbed and howled as I begged to be sent home. When my mother brought me back in the afternoon, the teacher decided not to take any chances and seated me in one of two individual desks off to the side, which, to my relief, remained my desk for the rest of the year.

Sitting at my desk in the front being very studious.

Despite my difficult first day, I loved school and was a good student. My younger brother Max joined me a year later, and we have many fond memories of those first few years. A not-so-fond memory sticks in my mind, though. One day a nurse came into the school to give the students a series of vaccinations. She and the teacher hung an olive green army blanket at the front of the room to provide a screen, and we were told to line up to get our needle. No one moved. I was terrified, like everyone else, but I didn't want anyone to know. Also, I wanted to get it over with. So I got out of my seat and marched to the front of the line, the first to get the needle. It hurt and I was scared, but I didn't let out a sound. My older sister Edna's class was in the room waiting their turn, and she said she will never forget the image of her little sister coming out from behind the blanket, eyes glistening but head held high and a smile on her face. She often says that she sees that day as a metaphor for how I have lived my life—that my pride and nerve give me the ability to fight through fear and do things even if they are scary. And I guess that turned out to be true.

Every other summer, we went to Newfoundland to visit our grand-parents for six weeks. In the early days we took the *Kyle*, a ship that carried passengers and freight along the coasts of Newfoundland and Labrador. The ship was designed to break through ice—an ongoing hazard along the coast. It was decommissioned many years ago, and now sits rather forlornly off the coast of Harbour Grace in Conception Bay.

What adventures we had on that ship. We met other children and ran up and down the decks while our parents sat in deck chairs and leisurely kept an eye on us. After a few years, affordable commercial flights became available, so we began to fly to the island. We'd land at St. John's airport and my father would hire a cab to take us "around the Bay." The Trans-Canada Highway had not yet been extended to Newfoundland, so we travelled on narrow dirt roads that wove along the coast, through picturesque fishing villages, up and down hills and over the barrens.

We were fascinated by the livestock, since there were no farm animals of any kind in Labrador. For us, it was like going to the zoo and seeing lions or tigers. We marvelled and pointed excitedly all the way. "Oh, look—cows! Goats! Horses!" We were scared to death of these beasts, fearing they'd eat us if we got too close. The local kids were bewildered by our reaction to these ordinary animals.

My father, with me sneaking
into the picture.

On those visits, we'd divide our time between Old Perlican and Bay de Verde, where we'd play with our cousins, Vivian and Janet, and Raymond and Don and Doug and Boyd. Our mother and grandmothers served up marvellous traditional Newfoundland meals of pan-fried trout and salmon with scrunchions, fish and brewis, Jiggs' dinners, pease pudding, blueberry buckle, figgy duff and fried cod tongues dipped in batter (yes, cods have tongues—big ones, too), homemade bread, bakeapple, and partridgeberry jam with thick clotted cream. There was always warm Orange Crush and Pepsi from Nanny Churley's pantry and delicious hard-as-rock homemade gingersnaps from Nanny Emberley's. We'd have the time of our lives for the summer, then go back to Labrador and back to school.

THREE

FIRST GLIMMERS

I GREW UP IN blissful ignorance of sex. No one in my family ever talked about it, and as a young teen, I had to pretend to understand dirty jokes.

What's worse than a piano out of tune? An organ that goes flat in the middle of a piece.

Do you think I got that? Not a chance. But I laughed along and pretended to. (Didn't we all at that age?) I tried to trick some of my more sophisticated girlfriends by telling the joke and hoping one of them would reveal the secret. It never worked, and it took me a few years before I finally figured it out.

My parents often took in teachers to board with us in our little house in Happy Valley. I remember the formidable Miss White, who wore red lipstick and spike heels. All the adolescent boys—not to mention their fathers—were gaga over her. One night after supper, my mother and Miss White were lingering over a cup of tea while I lurked in the hall, eavesdropping. They were talking about me and I heard Miss White ask whether I'd "blossomed into the flower of womanhood yet."

"What?" said my mother, who clearly didn't know what she was talking about. Neither did I, but I knew she was asking about something important.

"Has she started menstruating yet?" explained Miss White.

"Oh," said my mother. "No, she hasn't."

The flower of womanhood? What a lovely way to put it, I thought. I couldn't wait to blossom!

I did get a smidgen of sex education when I was about thirteen. Two of my girlfriends and I discovered that we could get into a little windowless shed just across the street from the school. It even had a rough plywood table and some chairs in it. We called it our clubhouse and met secretly there during lunch for several weeks. I was the instigator, with my drive to find out more about sex and menstruation. I had picked up some literature from our local nursing station—wildly titillating pamphlets that featured peculiar drawings and bewildering descriptions of female reproductive organs. The pamphlets had pastel blue and pink covers featuring clouds and butterflies, and were called things like "Growing Up and Liking It" and "You're a Young Lady Now." There were strange words like "hormones," "Fallopian tubes," "wombs," "ovaries giving orders," "linings of somewhat velvety material." I didn't realize it, but these brochures were produced by the makers of sanitary napkins and always ended with ridiculous flowery language describing their products. At the time, though, those words seemed magical to me.

It was pitch black in the shed, so we snuck candles and matches from home. Every day, Shirley, Phoebe, and I lit our candle, leaned in to peer at the mysterious illustrations, and took turns reading aloud. It all came to a halt one day when I leaned in too close while reading a particularly exciting bit, and we suddenly caught the distinct smell of burning eyebrows. I panicked and ran screaming out the door. We were discovered; the secret club was no more. A padlock soon appeared on the door of the shed, and I had a hard time explaining my singed eyebrows to my parents.

That same year, I finally got my period. I felt like I'd caught up with my friends, at last. Then came the ordeal of buying sanitary pads at the Hudson's Bay store, where everyone in the town shopped. God forbid that any male might see you buying a box of Kotex! The store-keepers even wrapped the boxes in plain brown paper in a bid to disguise them.

One day, a girl at school told me about tampons. I really wanted to try them because I hated the messy pads and the ugly belts that held them in place. She gave me one of hers. I didn't have the package with the printed instructions, but she tried to explain how to insert them. The problem was that I didn't yet know there was any place there to put things.

I did my best. In the morning, before school, I took the tampon out of its little cardboard container and placed it horizontally in the general area. I couldn't for the life of me figure out what else to do with it. It kept slipping out of place, but I somehow made it to school. At lunchtime, I was walking with a friend, trying to keep the thing positioned; the only way to do that was to take very short steps with my thighs pressed tightly together, which made we walk sort of pigeon-toed. My friends stared and kept asking me what the matter was. And sooner or later, it did fall out. The next time I used a tampon, I bought a box myself and read the instructions. I was surprised and rather mystified when I discovered what you could do with it.

The first time a man touched me in an intimate way was at the dentist's office at the air force base. Our father took us there because there were no dentists in Happy Valley. The dentist asked my father to come back in an hour. I was led into a little room and placed in a special chair that leaned all the way back. As he examined my teeth, he asked, out of the blue, "Don't you have a mother?" Bewildered and somewhat alarmed, I replied, "Yes, I do. Why?" Then he cupped his hand over one of my breasts, squeezed and jiggled it, and said, "She should get you a bra. Don't you people know anything?"

I was humiliated and frightened. I couldn't wait to get out of there. When my father arrived, I began to cry and told him I was never going back. He assumed it was because it hurt, and I didn't disavow him of that notion. I couldn't tell him or my mother what had happened. We just didn't talk about things like that.

Age 15—love the flip.

When it was time to go back again, I refused. This was out of character for me, so it surprised my parents enormously. However, I did need to get my teeth fixed, and finally, after my father offered to give me a whole dollar each time, I went back until the work was completed. But I kept my arms firmly folded over my chest while I was in the chair and convinced my father to stay in the adjacent room.

I still didn't quite know how babies were made. I had my first serious boyfriend the summer that I was fifteen. We were visiting my grandmother in Old Perlican, and Bobby was the doctor's son. We used to go up in the hills, lie under the hot sun, and neck. We were always fully clothed, and when he touched my breasts and the kisses got sizzling, I'd move the lower part of my body away so there was no contact. I was afraid I'd get pregnant if even our fully clothed pelvises touched.

When I was sixteen, I hung out with my best friends Cheryl, Elsie, Joan, and Terry. I was proud to be included because they were by far the most sophisticated girls in our school—sexy, savvy, and they dated GIs! My first GI boyfriend, a boy named Alan, was sweet and cute. He used to pick me up in his car outside the school at lunchtime, and we'd go to an isolated spot and neck. Then he'd bring me back to school and off I'd go, prim and proper, to my classes.

Then one day, I came home to find my mother in tears. "Marilyn, you've been going out with a GI and your father knows," she hissed. My father stormed into the kitchen, smacked me, and bellowed that I couldn't see the boy again. I went back to school, red-eyed and furious. My mother told me it was the school principal who had snitched. Not long after that I heard that Alan was seeing another girl in our class—the lovely, sexy Elaine. My heart was broken.

At the time, I thought I was the only one who didn't know anything about sex, which I later learned wasn't the case at all. When I was still busy figuring out how to use tampons, a friend from my class, whom I'll call Sally, got pregnant shortly after she started dating an older boy. She kept up a normal life, going to school and even participating in sports activities, until she was six months pregnant, somehow managing to hide the steadily expanding bump. When she finally faced reality and told her parents, they confined her to her room for the last three months of her pregnancy. She continued with her studies at home, and was allowed to go to the nursing station and to visit the minister. But she wasn't allowed to see her friends. After giving birth, Sally came back to school and everyone, including her, acted as if nothing had happened.

Sally and I have remained friends. Years after that teenage pregnancy, she told me what a horrific experience she'd had. She was intensely lonely and no one would tell her anything about what was happening to her body. She said she would lie awake at night terrified, wondering how the baby was going to get out of her stomach. When she went into labour on a freezing cold day, she was dropped off outside the hospital at the Canadian Forces base by her older brother and left on her own to go inside.

Even though she was crying, she was shunned by the medical staff, and after the birth, she was not allowed to see her baby. The nurses wouldn't even tell her whether it was a boy or a girl. The fact that she'd given birth to a daughter remained unknown to her until she was located and reunited with her grown-up child. To this day, I feel I let Sally down those many years ago. She never spoke of it, and I was too young to know how much she was suffering. None of us did.

In my senior year, I snuck out of the house more and more to go out with my friends. We were all dating GIs, and I fell into the most serious relationship I'd had, with tall, lanky Paul. I believed we were in love, and I thought he was going to take me to America (or to "the world" as the GIs called it) and marry me. Turned out, he was married already. After his stint was finished in Goose Bay, I never heard from him again. I was not alone in this regard. Many girls had their hearts broken by handsome young GIs who forgot all about them once they got home.

But more significant than the inept teenage sex were the annual high school speaking contests—one for boys and one for girls—sponsored by the Newfoundland and Labrador Rotary Club. The area of Happy Valley–Goose Bay, including the American and Canadian air force bases, held local contests and the winners went to the finals in St. John's.

My brother Max and I, both of us with the gift for the gab—a talent all of our siblings shared—were part of our school's debating club. I loved every aspect of debating, from researching complex topics in massive encyclopedias (no Wikipedia back then), thinking through the arguments, writing my speeches, and the thrill of the debates themselves.

Once, Max and I argued on different sides of a crucial issue: Should Labrador stay as part of Newfoundland or should it join Quebec? By the eve of the big debate, I had written and practised my arguments, but Max hadn't done a thing. In desperation, I dove into the encyclopedias and spent half the night writing his argument. The debate went well. I felt that my partner and I argued our side brilliantly. However, the judges thought that my brother made a more convincing case, and his team won. No one believed me when I said I wrote his speech, and he wasn't telling, at least not that night. (He loves telling that story now).

I won the local girls' Rotary contest and was particularly proud that I beat the stuck-up girls from the Department of Transport base and the American and Canadian military bases. With the help of Mrs. Hodge, a teacher I adored (I now realize she must have been a feminist!), I wrote an indignant, cheeky speech entitled "It's a Man's World" to deliver at the contest final in St. John's. I had been emboldened after finding a *Chatelaine* magazine in the loft of my grandparents' barn one summer and discovering the writings of Doris Anderson. She wrote about things I had never heard discussed, let alone seen in print: abortion, spousal and child abuse, lesbians, and equality for women and girls. Those articles were a turning point, and that speech was the first daring stand I took as a feminist—even though I didn't know it at the time.

I arrived in St. John's with my teacher, my speech memorized and ready to perform. I walked into a large room and was shocked to see that almost everyone there was a man. When my turn came to speak, I quickly had those men in the palm of my hand. They knew what I was saying was true. They chuckled appreciatively, but with the complacency of men who believed girls and women were charming but lesser human beings. Then I landed what I thought was a knockout blow: I noted that the winner of the provincial boys' speaking contest got a hundred dollars, a trophy, and a trip to Ottawa. The winner of the girls' contest got her moment of glory while being presented with a cheque and a trophy—that's right, no trip to Canada's capital city for her.

I made a stunning point and the room erupted. The men jumped to their feet and began to hoot and holler and tap their cutlery on their glasses. I was so startled that I got lost and ended up repeating a few lines. However, with the aid of my cue cards, I quickly found my place again and came to a triumphant ending. I sat down to great applause. I thought I couldn't lose. Then the girl from Labrador City got up and began her speech about Christianity and being a good girl. It was sweet and pure and oh so sincere. She won; I came in second.

Little did I realize how handy my orating skills and my willingness to speak truth to power would come later in my life.

FOUR

MY VERY NEW WORLD

MANY HIGH SCHOOL graduates from Happy Valley went on to study at Memorial University in St. John's, but by the time I was in my final year, I had decided to go to college in Ottawa. I wanted to get as far away from home as I could. In my senior year, the new high school I attended, Hamilton High, produced its first yearbook. I was proud to be its editor. The yearbook contains more than one reference to my urgent desire to escape. My favourite song was listed as "We Gotta Get Out of This Place" (by The Animals—I still remember all the words). On another page, there is a cartoon of my head coming out of a newly hatched egg with the caption "Let me out, let me out."

I was a restless teen growing up in an isolated Labrador town wait-ing for something to happen. I didn't know what that something was, but I knew it wasn't going to happen in Happy Valley. And though I didn't yet have any sense of who I was, I felt like I didn't quite fit in. The situation was all the more difficult because my father was very strict and rather to the right of the political spectrum. I wasn't sure what my values were, but I knew that they were different from his. As well, I just wanted to have fun. I wasn't allowed to do the things that normal teenage girls did, like date and wear lipstick. I did both, of course, but

Name: MARILYN M. CHURLEY
Proto: Mirror mirror on the wall
         Whose the fairest of them all-----CRACk
Born: Old Perlican, Nfld.
Age: 17
Nickname: Prudence
Favourite T.V. Program: The Fugitive
Favourite Song: We Gotta Get out of this Place
Favourite Saying: Thats not fair
Pet Peeve: Buck Owens
Ambition: Go to England
Probable Fate: Shell get there on A banana boat

My last year of high school. Pixie cuts were all the rage in 1966.

not without causing my mother a great deal of trouble as she tried to hide my activities from my father. Having to sneak around caused me a fair bit of anxiety, and I was forever fearful about what might happen when I got home.

It was 1966, and I guess it comes down to being my nascent feminism. The world was rapidly changing—I got a glimpse of that through the one TV station we got, even if *Hockey Night in Canada* games were broadcast a week after they'd taken place. We did get to listen to the games live on CBC radio, though, and more than one transistor radio was broken by being hurled across the room when my brother Max's beloved Toronto Maple Leafs lost. (No change there—I can still imagine broken radios accumulating all over his house.)

I wanted to start fresh and to be free to explore the world without restrictions and judgment. I really wanted to be in a big city where no one knew me. As it happens, I knew somebody in Ottawa and had heard good things about it. And it wasn't as daunting as, say, Toronto or Montreal. I told my father that's where I wanted to go, and to my surprise, he let me.

I didn't have an idea of what I wanted to do with my life. I just knew I wanted to leave home and be free of my parents' restrictions. I counted down the hours until I left, and when I got on that airplane, I never looked back. Arriving in Ottawa, I might as well have landed on Mars. It couldn't have been more different from Happy Valley, and that's just the way I wanted it.

It never crossed my mind to celebrate my newfound freedom by buying a bottle of booze, as some of my friends recounted doing when they were first on their own. Instead, I went out to buy something that I loved the taste of, but that was hard to come by in Happy Valley—one of those aerosol cans of whipping cream. I went into my room, locked the door, sat on my bed, and pumped every last drop into my mouth until the can was empty. Though I felt a little sick after, it was pure freedom.

In this new city, I realized I was restricted by my cultural ignorance. I lacked the all-important sense of style. I didn't know what music to like or what clothes to wear. I watched people carefully and listened to everything they said, hoping for clues on how to behave.

I moved into a house with some other students, and when it was my turn to cook, I was in a panic. Stuffed green peppers were on the menu; I had no idea what a green pepper was, and I sure wasn't going to ask. Fortunately, I was saved by a kind housemate who came shopping with me. In the produce section, he began picking through a bin of bell-shaped green vegetables I'd never seen before. Now all I had to do was figure out what I was supposed to stuff them with once we got home.

Shortly after I arrived in Ottawa, some young people invited me to a party. There I met an attractive young man named Mark. We began spending a lot of time together, and it wasn't long before he asked me to move into his house. I was going to classes by day and spending my evenings with Mark, and it seemed like there were parties every night. People were smoking dope, drinking a lot, and listening to music. This was all so new to me. When I was introduced to Bob Dylan's music, I had to hide my reaction. His peculiar nasal voice sounded to me like a screeching cat, and I was mortified that I wasn't cool enough to like it. But I was intrigued and, later, as I listened closely to what he was singing, I became a huge fan. Still am.

My relationship with Mark seemed to be going well, and I thought he really liked and respected me. One night during a never-ending party, after I had gone to bed because I had early classes the next day, I got up to go to the bathroom. The guys were around the corner in the hall where they couldn't see me. They were talking, not surprisingly, about sex. Mark was telling his friends about his little slut from Newfoundland and describing in excruciating detail the positions we supposedly did it in. His friends were all laughing appreciatively.

I was humiliated. I thought I was a nice girl, and I couldn't fathom how any man could think of me this way. I slunk back to my room, got dressed and, for the first time in my life, went out of my way to get drunk. The next day I told Mark that I had heard what he said and that he could try those imaginary positions with someone else from now on. I moved into a little hotel apartment with another student.

I also resolved as of that night that as long as people knew I was a Newfoundlander, I would never get any respect. In the 1960s, Newfoundlanders were still the butt of "Newfie" jokes that demeaned their intellectual abilities and even their moral standards. I often heard Newfoundland girls referred to as dim-witted sluts who were good for only one thing. I had naively thought I was immune from all of that because I didn't have a typical Newfoundland accent. The joke was on me.

That night I hatched a plan. I decided to tell people I was from England. I looked at a map and picked out a little town that few in

Canada would have heard of, so I wouldn't be asked questions about it. And overnight, I developed a crisp British accent.

Soon after, I met a very sweet young man from the Toronto suburb of Scarborough. He liked me and respected me from the get-go. Naturally, I was convinced that it was only because he believed I was from England and that if he found out where I was really from, he would walk away. After a while, he brought me to a big old house on Waverley Street in downtown Ottawa that turned out to be a student co-op. Most of the young people who lived there were involved in interesting projects and adventures. I was completely taken with them and their lifestyle. He let me share his room until eventually someone moved out and I took her place in a large room with two other women.

I met a woman there, Samantha (not her real name), who became an instant friend. The first time I saw her, she was reclining on a couch in the basement, modelling for one of our housemates who was an artist. I had never met anyone quite like her. To me, she resembled a goddess with wide-spaced green cats' eyes, long blond hair, and a gorgeous, curvaceous body. She was as smart as she was beautiful, and she seemed very mysterious and sophisticated. But she, too, came from a small town—in Saskatchewan—and had grown up as isolated and unsure of herself as I was. We discovered that we had a lot in common and became fast friends. It was a great and abiding friendship that would last until she died in 2014.

I shared a room with two other women at the Waverley co-op for a few months and then got a room of my own at the Argyle housing co-op downtown. The Argyle house was a whole other kettle of fish. At this dilapidated three-storey house, I finally realized what kind of social and political revolution I had landed in. Some of the people who lived there were students and some were not. Most of us had bedrooms with doors, but otherwise the house was well known as a crash pad. There were old couches draped in quilts and armchairs scattered here and there, lamps with shades covered in soft vibrant fabrics, candles everywhere, and colourful Indian bedspreads hung on walls and in doorways.

I was deeply affected by the people I met in Ottawa and the kinds of activities they engaged in. The left-wing counterculture of the Argyle residents attracted me right away, with its emphasis on equality and peace, affordable housing, and education for all. I knew I had found people who had the kind of values I believed in, and I found that I no longer had to hide my thoughts for fear of being censored or ridiculed. I became an instant left-winger. My perception of the world was irrevocably altered during my short stay in that house.

FIVE

THE WORST HAPPENS

AMANTHA'S BOYFRIEND was in the army and stationed in another province. But in the meantime, she had become involved with the handsome, eccentric artist who was painting her portrait when we first met. This led to disaster—and to one of my most disturbing encounters with the sex police, those who took it upon themselves to enforce how women should behave and determine how they would be punished if they stepped out of line.

I remember how scared Samantha looked when she told her housemates she was pregnant. We sat around the dinner table discussing how we were going to find the money to pay for an abortion. Samantha and I went for a walk later that evening. It was the dead of winter; snow was falling and the wind was howling. Samantha slipped on the ice and she just lay there awkwardly. For some reason, I started to laugh uncontrollably. I felt awful but I couldn't stop. As I held out my hand to help her up, my laughter turned to tears, and we stood there in the snow crying, with our arms tightly wrapped around each other.

I earnestly told her that she didn't have to go through with the abortion, that we could get an apartment and I would work and together we would take care of the baby. We were both all of eighteen, with no money and no support. She had no choice but to reject my offer. Years later, though, Samantha surprised me by telling me how much that offer had meant to her.

Abortions were illegal, a horrifically scary thing that only happened to other people. Providers were found through word of mouth; in this case, the information came from a student we knew, named Margaret, who had been an exotic dancer in Montreal. Hard as it was for us small-town girls to believe, her contact was connected to the Mafia. She told us that she'd learned that they controlled the "safe" abortion scene in Canada.

We had all heard horror stories about botched operations and infections that were left untreated because women were afraid to get medical treatment if something went wrong. So, Mafia or not, Samantha was going with what was deemed the safe option. Meanwhile her boyfriend Perry (not his real name) came to Ottawa, and she confessed to him what had happened. He accompanied her to Montreal. I was glad he did because it was clear that he loved her dearly, and I knew he would stay by her side and do anything to keep her safe.

Well aware of the medical and legal risks Samantha was taking, her friends were worried until she arrived safely back home. She remained pale and quiet for a few days, but then, as she began to recover and get back to normal, she had an incredible cloak-and-dagger story to tell.

Samantha had been directed to a nursing home. After she was examined, she was handed a piece of paper with a phone number on it and told to call the number from a specific phone booth at a specific time. She was warned to keep an eye out for the police, to leave immediately if she was approached by anyone, and to run away if she was even remotely suspicious.

Samantha made the call from a phone booth while Perry stood nervously by, keeping an eye out for suspicious-looking characters.

The person on the phone directed her to an ordinary apartment building, where she was instructed to go to a specific apartment alone. The abortion was performed on a padded dining room table. There was no anaesthetic, though Samantha was given a tranquilizer to keep her calm. She said the procedure was very painful, but she had been cautioned not to make a sound.

It meant a lot to Samantha that the nurse assisting the doctor was kind to her. The nurse gave Samantha some painkillers and, because it was freezing outside, warm pants to wear when she left. Samantha was told that if she had any problems, she should go to a hospital, but under no circumstances should she admit to anyone that she had had an abortion. My kind, gentle friend had become a criminal.

After what happened to Samantha, I was terrified of getting pregnant, so I went to a doctor to get birth control pills. After all, when it came to sex, guys were pretty irresponsible. They left it up to the girls to take care of birth control and often didn't even use a condom. The pill wasn't legalized for birth control in Canada until 1969, but a woman could get a prescription if it was needed to regulate her period. I wish I had known that at the time. I didn't know any doctors in Ottawa, so I asked someone for a referral. It turned out I should have been much more specific about what I wanted. I got an appointment with an older man who was both judgmental and prudish.

Never having been to a gynaecologist, I was nervous and uncomfortable, but I was also determined to take control of my own body. When I asked the doctor for a prescription for the pill, he refused because I wasn't married. He said he feared my taking the pill might make me promiscuous.

What the hell? That's exactly why I'm here, I thought, but I was too embarrassed to tell him that, by his standards, it was too late. I left, defeated and demoralized. Believing that any doctor would react the same way, I resolved that I would just have to be even more careful.

And I was until I met Chris. Chris, the drummer. Chris, the blue-eyed angel I fell for the moment I saw him. I met him in a coffee house in downtown Ottawa called Le Hibou, where all the hippies hung out and some of the best original music in Canada could be heard.

I spent a lot of time there because I was involved with others in the Argyle house writing and producing the first underground paper produced in Canada—*The Canadian Free Press*. The paper was started by two young men I greatly admired—Tony Seed and Steve Jones. The sign on the basement door that led to the grimy basement where the paper was produced, which you reached by rope ladder, read "Abandon Hope all ye who entre here." We spent hours talking about what the articles were going to be about, which was fascinating. I contributed some ideas, but at that point in my life I still mostly played a support role, typing and helping to distribute the paper.

As a pretty young woman, I'd be sent to Le Hibou and Café Le Monde to flog the papers. Not that I minded—I sold a lot of copies, and I also got to see fantastic performers like Bruce Cockburn, Joni Mitchell, Tim Hardin, David Wiffen, Colleen Peterson (who has since passed away), and other great local musicians, many of whom would end up at the Argyle house playing music until the wee hours of the morning.

One night, Chris dropped into the house after a gig. I had seen Chris many times playing drums in the cafés—he played with Bruce Cockburn in a band called The Children. I had developed a mad crush on him, but we'd never had a chance to hang out. That night, to my dismay, Chris was aloof and showed no interest in me. But after everyone went home or off to bed, I was surprised to see that he was still in the kitchen. Heading back to my room, I sprang into action. I took off my clothes and dressed in a bra and panties (modestly keeping on my half-slip), put a little speck of something in my eye, and went to the room he was crashing in. With tears streaming down my face,

I asked him to look in my eye to see if he could find what was in there and take it out.

This is how Chris looked when I met him.

That produced the close contact I wanted. We quickly fell for each other and were together every day from then on. But even though I adored him, Chris was curiously disengaged from the relationship, and we drifted apart. I didn't know then about the demons he was fighting and how mixed up and confused he was.

One day, seeking some normalcy and three square meals, I went to stay with old friends of my parents in suburban Ottawa. They had two young children, one of whom had a nasty stomach flu. The following day, the other child was sick. After eating a huge pancake breakfast, I was feeling a bit queasy myself, so I decided I'd better go home.

It was very hot out. The bus was packed and the air was stifling. I was sweating profusely and became more and more nauseated;

eventually I threw up my entire breakfast. In the heat, the stench was horrendous. The driver pulled over, and the passengers were let off to wait for another bus. He also called an ambulance, which whisked me off to the nearest hospital.

Soon after I arrived, the attending nurse looked me in the eye and said, "You know what's wrong with you, don't you, dear?"

"Yes," I groaned, "I have the stomach flu."

"No, dear, I think you might be pregnant."

I got all huffy and said I was sure she was wrong. I went for a pregnancy test at her insistence, but I was not worried. I had just had what I thought was my period. The results were a shock. It turned out that what I had had was known as a false period, something I'd never heard of, and—damn it all to hell—I was pregnant.

I was panic-stricken. My first thought was to kill that doctor who refused to give me birth control pills. My second was to jump off a bridge. A third, more realistic, thought was to do what Samantha had done and arrange an abortion.

Having the baby was not an option for me. I was deeply afraid of my father's anger, which would also have had repercussions for my mother. I could not have a child, and my parents could not ever find out that I was pregnant. End of story.

Margaret helped me make the appointment with the same doctor Samantha had seen. I was able to scrape together three hundred dollars from my friends and I set off for Montreal with Margaret and our friend Stephen. It was a surreal and terrifying experience.

We got there with time to kill, so we went to a movie. Then on the way to the appointment, I reached into my purse and discovered that my wad of bills to pay for the procedure was gone. I should have taken this as an omen and stopped right there, but instead we raced back to the theatre in a panic. In the dark, I crawled over people to get to our seats, and to the astonishment of those sitting there, scrambled on the floor feeling around for the money. To my immense relief, I found it, and with the bills clutched firmly in my hand, we set off once again.

The address was a rundown nursing home, no doubt the same one where Samantha had been examined. It smelled ghastly—a mixture of urine, grime, strong cleaning fluids, and stale food and bodies. The long, narrow hallway was painted a sickening institutional green. Frail, demented-looking old people were sitting around the reception area and in the hallway, some tied into their wheelchairs. They seemed to be staring at me as though they knew exactly why I was there—and no doubt, some did.

As I stood nervously at the counter, I thought I could hear them whispering and laughing at me behind my back. Everything seemed weirdly distorted and menacing. They were just old people in a substandard nursing home, but I was wracked by extreme fear and anxiety and I had never been exposed to conditions like these before. Even though the malevolence I felt was mostly conjured up in my mind, that scene nearly did me in and gave me nightmares for years.

I gave the receptionist the false name I had been told to use, and said I was there for a job interview with the doctor. After some time, a middle-aged man in a white coat called me in. I followed him into a room where he had me sit in a reclining chair and, in the guise of an examination, casually sexually molested me. Even now, I can barely bring myself to think about the probing, the confusion, the fear, and the humiliation. The professional accoutrements that help women in that exposed and powerless position maintain a sliver of dignity and control were not present. There was no gown to put on, no examination table to lie on, no stirrups to put my feet in, no protective sheet to drape over me. He was not wearing surgical gloves.

When he was done, he asked me how old I was and when I had had my last period. I told him I was eighteen, but I could tell by his sceptical look that he didn't believe me. I did appear much younger than my years, but there was no way I could provide him with ID; under the circumstances, I did not want him to know my true identity. He probably thought it was risky enough performing illegal abortions, but providing one for someone he believed to be under legal age was too big a risk to take.

At any rate, after all that, he told me he thought I was too far along for an abortion. When he was finished saying his piece and I started to protest, he turned his back and sent me on my way. I was in shock; now, all I wanted was to get out of there. I pulled my clothes together, running blindly out of the room, past the rows of old people staring at me, and stumbled out into the bright sunshine of the day. Margaret and Stephen came after me as I bolted from the place and kept on running until I couldn't run anymore. I fell to the sidewalk, shivering and gasping for breath. Then they were on the pavement holding me.

It was then that I made up my mind. I wasn't able to go through with an abortion after that experience. I would have the baby somehow or other without my parents and the rest of my family knowing.

SIX

NOW WHAT?

MARGARET, STEPHEN, AND I drove back to Ottawa. I had no clue what I was going to do. All I knew was that I was going to have a baby and I was on my own.

There was no way I could keep my baby unless I got married, which was not going to happen with Chris. I couldn't tell my parents; the disgrace would be too much. Being a single mom just seemed unacceptable and undoable. There were no supports. I was single, alone, and powerless; I had little money and no job. I didn't believe I had any option except to give my child up for adoption. That's what society expected.

Soon after arriving home from Montreal, I contacted Chris and told him I was pregnant. To my relief, he invited me to move in with him and his mentor. Unfortunately, this man, who called himself Mathew (not his real name), had delusions that he was the reincarnation of Jesus Christ. He didn't welcome my intrusion into their lives. He seemed to dislike women, or at least, it was clear he really hated me and wanted Chris all to himself.

Mathew was tall and thin and looked stern and serious all the time. He wore his hair and beard long and dressed in flowing white robes. Mathew and Chris used to drop acid and smoked marijuana constantly. They ate only macrobiotic food—mostly brown rice with sometimes a bit of miso thrown in for flavour. There was not much other food in the house.

Despite that, it was good to have a place to stay. Things were going reasonably well, given my now desperate straits. We had little to do with each other, but at night Chris would come to bed with me in his room. We talked and held each other, and he reassured me that everything would be okay.

But everything was not okay. Mathew told Chris that sleeping in the same bed with a woman—even with no sex—would hinder his spiritual progress, and Chris believed him. He stopped coming to bed with me, and I had almost no contact with him anymore. I was suffering from constant nausea. The smell of the rice made me ill, and I couldn't eat it. I got dangerously thin and weak, but I wasn't allowed to bring any other food into the apartment and I was too sick and miserable to go out.

I craved a bowl of hot soup. One day when I thought they were out, I scraped up enough change to buy a can of Campbell's vegetable soup, my childhood favourite. I hid it in my purse, entered the apartment, and furtively opened the can in the kitchen. The smell was tantalizing. I couldn't wait to savour it. I was just about to pour the soup into a pot when the door flew open and in strode Mathew, eyes blazing. It was as if he'd caught me releasing poison gas into the atmosphere. He leapt at me and angrily snatched the can out of my hands, turning it upside down and dumping the contents on the floor. He yelled incoherently about how dared I bring such impure food into his home. I stood there frozen with fear, expecting to be hit. He finally stalked out, still shaking with rage, and demanded that Chris come with him.

Chris did. I was left to clean up the mess. I scrubbed it on my hands and knees, bawling so hard that tears dripped into the ruined soup. I knew in that moment I had to get out of there—Mathew might physically harm me next. But I had no one to turn to and nowhere to go.

Samantha had moved to Victoria, British Columbia. Out of desperation, I phoned her to ask if I could come and stay with her for a while. To my relief, she agreed.

My parents thought I was still at school, and my letters gave no hint that something was terribly wrong. However, now that I was leaving Ottawa I had to tell them something. I wrote them that I was dropping out of college for a while to go to work and that a girlfriend in Victoria had found me a job. I don't think it came as a big surprise to them; they had always regarded me as the pretty one in the family, who would be best off getting married and raising a family.

I had placed myself in a difficult position financially. Now that my parents knew that I had dropped out and believed I had a job, I could no longer expect any money from them. I wanted it that way, though. I felt terribly guilty about the turn my life had taken and did not feel I could ask them to support me any longer. I would just have to find a way to get by on my own.

I survived the long bus trip from Ottawa and moved into a house Samantha was sharing with friends. It was a beautiful, rambling cottage just outside the city, surrounded by a colourful garden and with a little stream out back. We all got along just fine at first and I loved it there.

Samantha had a new boyfriend. He had a motorcycle and he took me on rides on country roads and rough terrain. I had read somewhere that jostling could cause a miscarriage so I kept urging to him to go faster and faster. But after a few weeks, he seemed to tire of my presence, and the tension was causing problems in my friendship with Samantha. I adored Samantha and did not want our relationship to deteriorate. It was clear that I had to move on.

I went into Victoria and threw myself on the mercy of the welfare office, but I got no relief there either. An intake worker gave me an ultimatum: they would give me assistance if I agreed to tell my parents I was pregnant and then only if my parents refused to help me financially. I was devastated to be given such a choice; it was really no choice at all. I pleaded with her to try to understand why I couldn't tell them, but she really didn't care. I collapsed in despair. Finally, she threw me a bone. She gave me a couple of names of families who were looking for pregnant girls to provide cheap labour in their homes.

Desperate for this chance to work out, I set off for my first interview to become a live-in housekeeper and nanny in a Victoria suburb. It did not go well. The woman spoke to me with contempt, indicating that I was lucky she was willing to do a favour for someone in my predicament. She spat out a list of my responsibilities—cleaning, laundry, preparing meals, taking care of the children—and told me there would be no pay, although room and board would be covered. Nothing in her words or tone showed any hint of human kindness. I was already so lonely and frightened. I just couldn't do it. Now I really had come to the end of the line.

In a state of shock, I walked around downtown Victoria for hours, wondering what I was going to do. Near tears, I took refuge in a movie theatre, sat in the back row, and quietly sobbed my way through the film. I don't remember what movie it was, but it featured a woman with closely cropped hair, kind of like Mia Farrow's in *Rosemary's Baby*. When I emerged into the bright daylight, I walked into the nearest hair salon and had my long hair cut off.

I returned to Samantha's house in the country with vague plans of returning to Victoria to see if I could get a job or find a home for unwed mothers. Samantha was aghast at my nearly shaven head, and told me I could stay a while longer while we figured something out. Then out of the blue, late in that summer of 1967, a miracle happened.

Samantha's former boyfriend, Perry, came to Victoria to see her. Shortly after Samantha had the abortion, she had broken up with him.

He was still in love with her and was hoping that she would come back to him. Samantha cared for Perry, but she told him that she had well and truly moved on and made it clear their relationship was over.

Perry and I started spending a lot of time together, mostly talking about Samantha and about the difficult situation I was in. Because he was still in the army, he had only a few days before his next stint at the base at Camp Borden near Barrie, Ontario. He invited me to live with him until after the baby was born; in exchange, I would do housework and cook. I was saved.

I arrived in Barrie within days and we rented a pretty little converted coach house. Perry was a good man and, although he was still broken-hearted, he and I developed a warm, loving relationship. We became lovers during the months we lived together, and the neighbours thought we were husband and wife. What an odd couple we made. I was barely five foot two and looked about fifteen. Perry was six foot four and looked older than his twenty-four years.

Perry had become disillusioned with the army and wanted out. We became friends with a group of progressive students living in a big house near the art gallery in downtown Toronto, and we visited them almost every weekend. There I met Lesley, a bright, articulate, and kind person who was a couple of years older than I was. And we had something important in common—she was pregnant, too. When she'd learned she was pregnant, she'd married the father of the baby. It was not a good match, and she knew she had made a mistake. We became very close friends and still are today. But there was a big difference between us. She was going to be able to keep her baby, and I was going to have to give mine away.

SEVEN

IN HOSPITAL, ALONE

I **WAS PRETTY HAPPY** in the coach house in Barrie. As the months went by, I got bigger and bigger and the baby became more and more active. In many ways, we lived the life of a normal couple expecting a baby in those days. Perry went to work every morning and I stayed at home. I wasn't a great cook by anyone's standards, but I took my part of the bargain seriously. Every night he'd come home to dinner on the table, the beds made, and the apartment clean and tidy.

In the evenings we read and Perry practised his guitar. Perry was good to me in many ways. I would have cravings for cream soda and once he got up in the middle of the night to get me some.

I contacted the Children's Aid Society about giving my baby up for adoption, and they sent a young social worker to start the process. She was kind and gentle and appeared to truly care about my wishes for my baby. She became my only contact in Barrie other than Perry, and I came to view her as my friend and confidante and to look forward to her visits. As we filled in the forms together, she asked me a lot of details about my background. To my surprise, she wanted to know my preferences for the adoptive family. I insisted that I did not want my baby to go to an overly religious and strict home. That was the way I had been brought up; I wanted my baby to live in a more broad-minded, tranquil environment.

By Christmas, my tummy was huge. Appearing much younger than my years, I looked like a little girl with a beach ball stuffed inside her clothes. But for trouble sleeping and constantly having to pee, I was in good health. Part of me was desperate for the birth so I could have my body and my life back. But I also dreaded the day I would lose my precious child. The child I called Andrew and talked to and sang to all day. The child that was such a part of me, the child I had come to love.

And I was thinking of something else. Perry and I were living together happily and it seemed logical to me that we get married and keep the baby. Perry didn't see it that way, though.

I began to notice letters coming from someone in Calgary, and Perry would stay up late some evenings writing letters back. I asked him who she was and he told me he had met someone at a conference; they liked each other and had agreed to write and get to know each other better. I was home alone all day and was so worried that, though I felt guilty about doing it, I steamed open her letters as they arrived. Not nice, I know. But desperate people sometimes do desperate things. To my dismay, I discovered a budding romance was going on, at least on paper. I couldn't say anything to him and I persuaded myself that, since he hardly knew this girl, in the end, he would change his mind and agree to stay with me and keep the baby.

By late January, I was two weeks past my official due date. It was very hard to sleep and to get around. I was a wreck, though I loved the feel of that baby kicking and moving around inside me.

On January 29, my water broke, and as I started to feel mild contractions, Perry took me to the hospital. He didn't stay with me; I didn't know that I could ask him to. Besides, it wasn't his baby and he was on his way to work. On top of that, neither of us knew what a hard time I was in for. I had spent my pregnancy in a state of ignorance.

I had no female friends in Barrie, and my doctor was not very forthcoming about birthing techniques. No one in my family, including my brothers and sisters, knew about the baby or even where I was living. I needed my parents to believe I was still in British Columbia, so once a week I wrote a letter to them telling them all about my friends, my adventures, and my job, and mailed it off to Samantha in Victoria, who in turn mailed it to Labrador. This simple scheme to keep them in the dark worked just fine.

So there I was, nineteen years old, alone in a hospital about to give birth. A nurse gave me a hospital gown and put me in a small, cheerless room that had only a bed and a big, round wall clock. Tick-tock, tick-tock... From the time they put me in that bed it was a hellish twenty-four hours before my baby was born. I had no book or magazine, no television or radio, no company. After I changed into the gown, a nurse, to my consternation, gave me an enema. This was bad enough, but I really freaked out when she shaved my pubic area—a common practice at the time—and wouldn't explain why.

I was so afraid. Why would none of the nurses say something to me to alleviate my fear? How could these women, many of whom would have given birth themselves and some of whom probably had daughters my age, be so unkind to me? Such was the attitude toward unwed mothers that even nurses, generally so caring and compassionate, seemed to think it was okay to treat me harshly.

Occasionally, one of them popped in to check on me, while for hours, I could hear shattering screams coming from down the hall that frightened me even more. As my contractions came closer together, the pain got out of control and I joined the chorus of screams. No one had told me it would be this bad. I was not given an epidural, nor was it even mentioned as an option. I would have accepted one in a heartbeat.

Finally, I was moved to another room and onto the delivery table. By this time, I was drenched in sweat, exhausted, and having unbearably painful contractions. I had no idea that this was the way it went in the final stage of birthing. I was so frightened I thought I was dying.

I cried out in pain. My feet were placed into stirrups. The doctor arrived, cold as ice, offering no compassion, no reassurance. My natural instinct to run from a traumatic situation overtook me and I tried to jump off the table. The nurses held me down. The doctor barked that if I didn't behave myself, they would tie me to the delivery table. I held still then, the idea of being restrained scaring me more than anything.

The pain lessened and I was told to push. I pushed hard, wanting so much for this to be done. Finally, I heard a cry—and it was over. A nurse cut the cord, wrapped my seven-pound, nine-ounce baby boy in a blanket, and turned to hustle him out of the room.

"I want to hold my baby!" I screamed, despite my exhaustion. They ignored me. The nurse was almost out the door, when, with a surge of energy, this time I did leap off the delivery table and I ran after her. "I want to see my baby!" The nurse spun around and said if I got back on the delivery table, she would bring him to me. I got back on the bed and she held him close to my face. I reached out to take him in my arms, but she shook her head sternly.

Fresh from my body, he was covered with mucus and blood and crying heartily. But I had never seen anything so beautiful in my life. I reached out and caressed his head. And that was it. The nurse whisked him away.

By then I was too tired and overcome with emotion to protest. I was wheeled into a semiprivate room, which surprised me because I did not have health coverage for that. A young woman slept in the other bed, and I, too, soon fell asleep.

I woke up to hear my roommate crying. My heart leapt because I thought she might be in the same position I was; at least I would have someone to commiserate with. I introduced myself and asked if she was okay, but she turned her back on me and didn't speak. Later, I asked a nurse what was wrong. She told me that the woman's husband had recently been killed in a car accident, and that was why we had been separated from the other mothers.

I couldn't understand the connection at first, but then it dawned on me that we were both viewed as sad women who'd had babies in tragic circumstances and they wanted to keep us away from the happy mothers. At any rate, the young widow appeared to resent being lumped in with an unwed mother, and although I wanted to be sympathetic to her, she continued to behave as though I didn't exist.

The next day, I persuaded the head nurse to move me to the larger ward with the other new mothers. It was a difficult scene for me to observe: new moms happily cradling their babies; husbands and family members bringing gifts, flowers, support, and love. But at least they were too wrapped up in their own bliss to be openly hostile toward me.

At every chance, I raced down the hall and stared longingly through the nursery window at my little boy, whom I had called Andrew. He looked so tiny and lonely in his little bassinet, but the nurses wouldn't let me inside the nursery or even bring him closer to the window. I didn't question them; I was too naive to know that they had no legal right to prevent my access to my own child.

At that time, women were kept in hospital for up to a week after having a baby, so I had to endure having my baby just down the hall but out of bounds to me. I thought I would go crazy. So that my breasts would stop producing milk, I was given a breast pump and my breasts were then tightly bound. I was also given some vile-tasting black pills to help speed things along. Perry came to visit me in the evenings. I begged him to change his mind and stay with me so we could keep the baby, but the answer was still no.

The night before I left the hospital, I dreamt I was holding my baby. I was breastfeeding, feeling warm and contented. All was right with the world. Then, out of nowhere, a fairy-tale hag approached the bed. Dressed in black with a shawl over her head, she approached me slowly with her arms held out. I recoiled in terror as she reached out to take my baby.

I woke up screaming. A nurse ran in and I told her through my sobs about the witch who came to take my baby away. She scolded me for making such a racket and waking up the other patients, gave me a sleeping pill, and told me to go back to sleep.

That was the prevailing atmosphere in the hospital. I was treated badly by almost everyone. One nurse came to my bed and slipped a plain gold band in my hand, whispering that I should wear it so that people would think I was married. I said no and her eyes went cold. "Fine," she snarled. "You should be ashamed of yourself. I was trying to help you, but you are nothing but a shameless little hussy." As she turned and stalked away from me, I cried out, "I am frightened and sad, but I am not ashamed!" That nurse became the most hostile of them all.

Three years later, in 1971, I would hear Joni Mitchell's beautiful song "Little Green." I was captivated by her sad and haunting tone and by the first line in the song, "Child with a child pretending." But I couldn't believe my ears when I heard her sing "You're sad and you're sorry but you're not ashamed." I knew what those words were about, and I knew that what happened to me had happened to Joni, too.

The morning after my wretched nightmare, I was discharged from the hospital. It was the day I said goodbye to my baby. Perry took the morning off work to pick me up. I took my last walk down the corridor to the nursery and asked—begged, really—if this time, I could please, please go in and, if not hold my baby, be allowed to see him without a layer of glass between us. The answer was the same: no. They said that I would be leaving soon and I had to go away and forget about ever having had this baby so I could start afresh and get on with my life. Holding him would make that more difficult, the nurses said. Perhaps they thought this was an act of kindness, but it seemed cruel to me.

But my begging forced a compromise, and they pulled his bassinet close to the window and, at my request, removed his little blue blanket. He was lying there wide awake, wearing just a diaper. I was as close as I could get, face pressed up against the glass, staring into his blue eyes, and he seemed to be staring back just as intently. I took in every ounce of him, trying to memorize his features.

"Goodbye, little Andrew—for now. I love you and one day I will find you," I whispered.

The nurse wheeled away the bassinet as tears streamed down my face. Overcome with longing and grief, I felt broken beyond repair.

Perry got to the hospital later than planned, so I was waiting by the door for him. This turned out to be not a good thing, because I had checked out and the staff thought I was gone. As Perry and I were leaving, I spotted my social worker coming down the stairs holding a little blue bundle. I knew it must be my baby and, in a moment of panic and disorientation, I thought someone was stealing him. I pulled away from Perry and started after her. Perry virtually dragged me away.

In the car, I came to my senses. But I felt something tighten inside me and a cold chill go down my back. I knew then that I would never be the same again.

At home, I was inconsolable. I felt unbearable sorrow, and despite the pills, and no matter how much I pumped, I had full, tender breasts that constantly leaked milk. I was shattered, both physically and mentally. Perry bought me a case of cream soda to cheer me up. I at least felt secure in that I still had a lover and friend to help get me through this. Against all odds, I held on to the hope that he would change his mind and marry me and I could get my baby back.

~

PART II

THE ELEVATOR LADY'S SON

EIGHT

THE DREAM IS OVER

OH, HOW MISERABLE was that first night home from the hospital. My baby was gone. I never even got to hold him, to kiss him good-bye. I was so low, I didn't think things could get any worse.

Exhausted, I went to bed early. I tried to stay awake waiting for Perry to join me. I needed to be held, to be comforted. I drifted off. When I woke up after midnight to find the bed empty, I went to the kitchen to look for him. Perry was at the dining table, writing. I startled him and he looked uncomfortable as he tried to conceal some papers.

"Perry," I asked, "what's going on?" He said he was writing his mother and was almost done. He put the letter away, came to bed, and soon fell asleep. But knowing something was up, I couldn't fall back to sleep. I crept out to the kitchen and found the letter stuffed in a book on the table. My hands shook as I picked it up.

"Dear Judy [not her real name], Marilyn had her baby and it has been adopted so soon she will be gone and I will be free for us to get together." He went on about how hard it had been holding off all those months because of his obligation to take care of me until the baby was born, about how he had fallen in love with her though their correspondence and telephone conversations. It was all very tender and sweet.

I was left reeling. Perry had been happily sleeping with me while this romance was starting to bud. And hard reality hit me: there was no chance I would get my baby back. I just had to get away from him. Ready to run, I started to dress. But I was too sore and tired. I knew, though, I'd leave the next day. Exhausted as I was, I hardly slept as I thought about what I was going to do.

Perry got up early and found me on the couch. I was clutching his letter in my hand, so he knew that I knew. I had already decided to take up my friend Margaret's invitation to stay with her and her boyfriend in New York City. Perry bought my airline ticket and gave me some money to help me get back on my feet. He drove me to the Toronto airport and we said a sad goodbye.

It was a frigid February. Margaret, the friend who had come with me to Montreal the year before, was a stunning beauty. Andrew, an underground filmmaker, was a big handsome man with flowing hair. They lived in a sprawling walk-up over a store at Houston and Avenue A. It was kind of a rough area, so there were multiple locks up and down the door. They kept the place beautifully furnished with stuff plucked from the curbside on garbage nights in posh areas of town.

I walked every day for miles and miles, trying to soothe the ache in my heart. I loved New York; I could just get lost in it. I was so traumatized by everything that had happened with the baby and Perry that only a part of me was there, but that's why the big city was perfect. Through Margaret and Andrew, I met all kinds of alternative filmmakers, artists, actors, and other odd characters who made up the underground scene.

But amid all of that, I was very depressed. I wanted just one thing: to return to Toronto to get my baby back. Andrew and Margaret were very kind and supportive, and they did their best to cheer me up. But nothing worked. One day, Andrew suggested that he come with me to Ontario; together, we would get my baby and bring him back to New York.

I jumped at the offer. When a child was relinquished to adoption, the birth mother had three months in which she could change her mind and reclaim the baby. It was only February; I still had plenty of time.

But Margaret, being the pragmatic one, talked us out of it—or at least talked Andrew out of it. I couldn't blame her for not wanting the responsibility of housing a single mom and a newborn. She also persuaded me that it might not be the best thing for me and the baby, anyway. I knew she was right, so with heavy heart, I went back to the freezing streets of New York for hours on end. I picked up odd jobs—delivering flyers or doing grocery shopping for shut-ins. Then I would go back to the flat, listen to music (mostly Leonard Cohen—I think he saved my life) and cry. One of my favourite songs was "One of Us Cannot Be Wrong" from *Songs of Leonard Cohen,* his first album. It's the one that starts: "I lit a thin green candle, to make you jealous of me. / But the room just filled up with mosquitos, they heard that my body was free."

New York was all about getting through those three months. I didn't think about what I would do with the rest of my life. I just tried to get through each day, and Margaret's was a very comforting place to be. I am grateful for her love and support during that dreadful period.

I still spoke to Perry on the phone almost every day. He was now in Toronto, having left the army, and was waiting for his pen lover to arrive. One day, out of desperation, I called him and begged him to let me come back and live with him, at least until Judy got there. He didn't sound too happy, but he reluctantly agreed.

When I told Andrew and Margaret what I was about to do, Andrew gave me some advice. He said that if I wanted to get Perry back, I had to play hard to get. Going back to him while he was waiting for another woman would ruin any chance that he would see me as strong and desirable. And even though I was not okay, I had to pretend that I was. Andrew was very persuasive. I realized that I would lose my self-respect if I went back under those circumstances.

I called Perry the next day and told him I had changed my mind. I said that I had called him in a moment of weakness, but was feeling stronger every day and would not be coming back. To my surprise, Perry sounded disappointed and tried to convince me to come. Andrew had been right, and I was gratified.

Perry and I corresponded during that time, and I still have most of his letters to me as well as some that I wrote to him and never mailed. I am astounded by the near absence of any reference to my baby. His letters were full of confusion and ambiguity about his feelings for Judy and me. He only referred to the baby once in response to something I had said about the profound effect losing my baby was having on my life. In a letter of mine, I put on a humorous, almost jaunty style to give some details of how my body was healing. I wrote that it was all good—everything was almost back to normal, and although I would never quite have my eighteen-inch waist back, I was thanking my lucky genes that I didn't have any stretch marks and that you'd never know that I had had a baby.

The thing is, though, the few things I did write about the baby were penned in tiny cramped writing on a blank page isolated from all the other news—like furtive whispers that can barely be heard. I guess I was already beginning to feel that I should not talk about this anymore.

It would be easy to write Perry off as an insensitive cad who used me, but that was not the case. In fact, he is one of the finest men I've ever known. He was a product of his time, as was I; together we carved out a path through some difficult situations. Despite how badly it ended, I look back at those few months in Barrie as a time of great comfort, support, and love. He was young and confused and, like most young men of that era, caught between an emerging view of equality in relationships between women and men and the old attitudes where men were in control. On top of that, he was heartbroken over his breakup with Samantha, and he, too, needed companionship and love. We had made a bargain that was convenient for both of us, and I had, at least on the surface, agreed to it.

Perry had made it clear from the get-go that he was not committing to me beyond the birth of my baby. I was having a baby in secret, and he was willing to take care of me until it was over. I knew this full well as we fell into an intimate relationship. But we didn't realize the complexities of that bargain. I convinced myself that the relationship was more than that, but I had to accept the reality of his uncertain feelings for me. We were in the most unequal of relationships, and there was no way that he could see me as an equal partner until that phase was over.

After my talk with Andrew, it began to dawn on me that I was on my own and that I needed to go home and get on with my life. It finally hit me. It's all gone. The baby's gone, Perry's gone. I've got to move on.

I came back to Toronto and moved in with my friend Lesley and her sweet baby girl, Lyndsay, who was just a few months younger than my son. I still thought of my missing child all the time, but the three-month grace period was over. I had to let him go.

Meanwhile, the pen lover had come and gone, as I had expected. Perry now realized he was in love with me, and pursued me aggressively upon my return from New York. We tentatively started our relationship over on a new footing. I was still keeping a distance from my family, so they did not factor much into my life at the time. (It was 1968, remember—no internet, no cell phones. We wrote letters on paper and put them in the mail!)

I was able to share my life with Perry, without revealing much about my family. He still thought I was from England. I was pretty good at changing the subject whenever my homeland came up, but once I almost got caught out.

Perry was reading to me in bed (a nice habit we had adopted in Barrie) and the book's plot was set in Britain. There was a mention of ha'pennies and shillings, and Perry asked me how much that was in dollars. I didn't have a clue; my research into England hadn't quite gone that far. Instead of answering, I dashed to the bathroom complaining of stomach pain. I stayed in there moaning for a while, and by the time I came out feeling all better, Perry had forgotten all about currency conversion.

I picked up the pieces of my life and began working as a temp for a government agency. Eventually Perry and I got together as a real, honest-to-goodness couple. He now realized he had been in love with me all along, and he asked me to marry him. I knew then that I would have to tell him where I was from, but I was sure that once he found out I was a Newfoundlander, he'd call it off.

Now, isn't that insane? Today I find it hard to comprehend how absurd it was for me to believe I was unworthy to be married to a "Canadian." It just shows how deep bigotry cuts into our souls. And I was a white woman of privilege; my experience doesn't come close to the racism that Aboriginal people and people of colour experience. Although it was a silly thing to do, I had been able to hide my "shameful" roots. But the experience left a bitter taste and had a lasting impact on my self-esteem.

I kept putting off telling Perry where I was from even after we had our marriage licence, a date set, and a minister ready to perform the ceremony. The day was fast approaching and I still had not told him. Perry had left the army and was now teaching at the University of Toronto's Scarborough College, east of the city. We lived downtown, so he drove out there every day in our white second-hand Volkswagen Beetle—one of those bugs with a big flower painted on the side. One day, I told Perry I was taking the day off work and was going to drive out with him. I had decided I would tell him during the ride to campus.

I dressed for the occasion. I wore a fedora hat and big sunglasses, so my face was partially hidden. We hadn't gone far when I said: "Perry,

I came with you today because I have something important to tell you." I stopped there. I couldn't do it. "It's bad," I cried. "Once you know you will not want to marry me."

"For God's sake, just tell me," Perry begged. But I just couldn't say the words. This went on all the way out there. He clutched the wheel tightly, looking hunched over and agitated—and no wonder.

"Tell me," he begged. "It can't be all that bad."

My heart pounded and my throat closed up, and with every attempt to speak I pulled my hat further down over my face and sank lower in my seat. We were almost on the campus—I had to tell him now. I girded myself. "I'm not really from England, I'm from Labrador," I whispered in a rush. I waited for the cry of horror.

"Oh my God, is that all!" He was crying and laughing so hard he had to pull the car off the road.

He reached over, took my hat off, and pulled me across the gear-shift to hug me tight. "Marilyn, you scared the shit out of me. I thought you were going to tell me you were an axe murderer or were dying of cancer, or something horrific. You didn't honestly believe I wouldn't marry you because you were from Labrador, did you? I love you. It doesn't matter where you're from. And I never met anyone from Labrador before. I think that is really cool." He may even have said "far out."

We both cried as I told him the story of the guy in Ottawa, and that I figured no man would want me if he knew I was from Newfoundland.

Sadly, the marriage was not destined to survive. In our initial relationship, we had gone through an intense experience together, but by the time we were married, we acted as though it had never happened. This gap was a constant companion in our relationship. I felt extreme regret that, after all we'd been through together, here we were married anyway and my baby wasn't with us. And the truth is, on some deep level, I was unable to completely forgive him.

NINE

A STAR IS BORN

ERRY AND I headed to Europe in the fall of 1970 for what was planned as an extended tour together. Instead, we parted ways shortly after we arrived, and I spent more than a year travelling around the continent and North Africa. Then I returned to Toronto and continued working as a temp for government agencies.

I also got more politically active, resuming an involvement in acting and the antiwar movement that had begun before I went away. The plays always had political and feminist themes. I was also involved in a lot of student and academic life, even though I wasn't a student. Through Perry, I had become friends with University of Toronto students and professors, mostly in psychology, which was a base for much of the counterculture movement. Many of us remained friends long after Perry and I separated.

While living with friends in a big old house on Hazelton Avenue, I fell head over heels for a handsome dude named Jon. He arrived at the house one day looking for a friend who used to live there. There was an instant spark between us. We talked at the kitchen table for hours. Jon was smart and funny. He was a certified plumber, though when I met him, he had become a free spirit who worked as a promoter for musical events.

In 1973 something totally unexpected happened. I was pregnant again. I was twenty-five years old, and most assuredly had not planned this pregnancy. After my first pregnancy, I found that taking birth control pills made me sick so I used an IUD instead. It was an early version of the device, which turned out to be defective and led to catastrophic medical repercussions. Along with thousands of other women, I ended up with a painful condition that caused inflammation of the reproductive organs. I was told that because of scarring caused by the constant inflammation, I would most likely never be able to conceive again.

The year after my son was born.

Part of me was actually okay with this news. On a certain level, I didn't think I deserved to have another baby after giving up my first. In fact, studies show that a large proportion of women who give up a child to adoption do not have any further children. But when I learned I was pregnant, after getting over the shock, I found myself very, very happy. Even though my baby's father was not the most suitable parent in the world, it was okay. I was mature enough to have this baby and, if need be, raise the child on my own. I might not get another chance.

Jon and I moved to Montreal, where he worked in the music business and I stayed home. We lived in a spacious but inexpensive apartment in the Saint-Henri neighbourhood with our friend Frank, an artist who designed record album covers. We didn't have a lot of money, just enough to live comfortably. We made friends with many musicians and artists, and our home was always full of people, music, and laughter.

The contrast with my pregnancy six years earlier was remarkable. This baby that was developing in my body would continue to be nurtured and loved by me after she was born. I joyfully went shopping for a crib, stroller, and blankets, booties, bonnets, and bottles. I shared the experience with Jon, who was thrilled at the notion of becoming a daddy. Together we talked about names and planned for the day the baby would come home with us.

Jon came to the hospital with me when my water broke and was with me throughout the birthing ordeal. He held my hand, wiped the sweat from my brow, and joked and cried with me when the pain became unbearable. I am quite sure he was massively stoned through it all. Jon was a great looking man—slim and muscular, with long blond hair. He was intense and self-confident, very charming, a bit rough around the edges—the perfect bad boy. The nurses all adored him.

The first time I was pregnant, I had been decidedly uninformed. But this time, I'd done my research. I knew I could have an epidural if I asked for one, but I decided to have a natural childbirth—for the good of my baby. Dumb decision. Come the unbearably painful transition stage, I cracked and asked for drugs—any drugs. And the sooner the better. By that time, it was too late for an epidural. The nurse gave me something to take the edge off that made me slightly stoned. I was lying there, panting and sweating and swearing with great gusto, and there was Jon on one side of the bed holding my hand, a sweet young nurse on the other side holding my other hand. They seemed to be flirting, but I didn't care one bit.

My little girl emerged into the world on March 24, 1974, and this time—oh, joy—the medical staff put the little mucus-covered creature on my stomach as they cut the umbilical cord. They placed her gently in my arms. I held her close, staring at her tiny, sweet face and her little squashed, hairless head. Jon sat with me and together we gently patted and stroked her and marvelled at how perfect she was.

We still hadn't decided on a name. My heart had been set on a girl, but I didn't want to jinx it by picking out girls' names or buying pink clothes. Instead, we had chosen boys' names and bought yellow clothes. I never said it out loud, but I knew I wanted a girl so badly because I didn't want to replace the son I had already had and lost.

I hadn't been in touch with my parents much in the years between the birth of my first child and the birth of my second. I had flown to Labrador to visit a couple of times and had taken Perry to Goose Bay to meet them and to Old Perlican and Bay de Verde to meet other members of my family. But after my daughter was born, I suddenly saw my parents in a different light. Lying in my hospital bed, my tiny new baby nestled in my arms, I phoned my mother. I was very emotional, telling her how now that I had a baby, I understood what it was like to be a mother. I thanked her for everything she had done for me and told her I was sorry for all the trouble I had caused her as a teenager. She seemed a bit flummoxed by my outburst, but I felt that she appreciated it. She was happy about the birth of her first grandchild and said that she couldn't wait to see her. I almost blurted out that in fact this was not her first grandchild, but I held my tongue.

Soon after the baby was born, I went to Montreal city hall to register the birth. I stood in line and, when my turn came, gave the clerk the application form I had filled in with my baby's name—Astra (Greek, meaning like the stars) Churley (my maiden name). I had put Jon's full name in as the father. However, even though Perry and I had been apart for four years, we were still married and I had legally changed my name to his. Back in 1969, I had thought it was mandatory to take your husband's name, so my name was listed with his surname, now my legal name, on the application form.

The clerk smelled a rat. He looked suspiciously at the application. "Who's Churley?" he asked. "Why, it's me!" I proudly proclaimed, producing my birth certificate. He promptly told me that Quebec law did not permit me to give my child my maiden name.

"In that case, she will be given her father's surname," I said. He told me I couldn't do that either. Under the law, I had to give her the name of my husband. I protested, explaining that although I was not divorced, I had not lived with my husband for years and obviously did not want my daughter to carry the name of a man with whom she would never have any connection. But the law allowed me no other choice.

The ordeal wasn't over yet. He then told me that if the father was not present to sign the document, the mother had to produce a witness to verify that the newborn was really hers. I patiently explained that here I was with the baby in my arms and I was the one who had just given birth. Why wasn't my signature good enough? "The law's the law," he replied.

"But," I said, near tears, "I didn't bring anyone with me." I badly needed to get this procedure completed that day. I was worn out and couldn't imagine going through it all again. The clerk, taking pity on me, suggested that I go into the hall and ask someone in line to volunteer to be my witness.

I was the mother! I had the baby in my arms! And this man was telling me that if the father were there he could have signed, but without him, I could only register my baby with a stranger as a witness.

I went out into the hall and approached a sad, elderly man waiting on a bench. I shyly explained to him what was going on and asked if he would witness the registration of my baby. The light in his eyes

and the smile on his face almost made the fiasco worthwhile. It turned out he was there to register the death of his wife, and he told me that the opportu- *In 1974 with my new daughter, Astra. I've come a long way from the pixie cut!*

nity to witness a new life was an amazing gift from God and that I had made his day. We went in together and, although this witness had known me for about sixty seconds, the clerk accepted his signature. Off I went with my now legal baby, with a surname that meant noth- ing to her. But now, at least, I could apply for the government baby bonus cheques.

I had the chance to do everything right with this baby. I began breastfeeding her right away. It cost me many sleepless nights, but it was worth it. She started walking at nine months and was stubborn as hell, and would grow into a charming, articulate, and sociable little girl.

As I cared for my baby girl, I kept on listening to Leonard Cohen's songs, the ones I had listened to over and over after I lost my son. I had a nightly routine of singing Astra to sleep for the first few years of her life. (I admit I sang that "thin green candle" song, but that was before she could understand the morbid words.)

I would rock her gently to sleep as I sang a chant I had learned from a Buddhist priest shortly after coming back from New York. Still disconsolate over the loss of my son, I'd gone to hear the priest speak, hoping he would say something that would help settle my heart. At the end of his talk, he led the audience in a chant and as I sang, the words soared straight from my heart to my lost baby: "Listen, listen, listen to my heart song—I will never forget you. I will never forsake you, I will never forsake you, I will never forget you." As I sang to my daughter, I was singing a goodnight song to my son, as well.

I have read that mothers who have given up their first child for adoption worry more than other parents about losing their second child—the one that they keep. That was certainly true for me. I loved my daughter so much—too much, perhaps. I never wanted to let her out of my sight, and she was on my mind all the time. I lived in a constant state of anxiety. I feared every second that something would happen to her—like she'd stop breathing out of the blue or be snatched from her cradle when I was sleeping.

When Astra was eighteen months old, we moved to Vancouver. Unfortunately, shortly after arriving there, I had to say goodbye to Jon. We'd tried hard to keep it together, and although he loved his daughter dearly and we loved each other, he was just not the type to settle down and live the kind of domesticated life that I wanted for our child.

Shortly after arriving in Vancouver, I enrolled at Simon Fraser University. My friend Samantha was now a graduate student at the same school. Things had not worked out for her in Victoria and she had returned to Ottawa shortly after I left for Barrie in 1967. There she'd met up with some of our old gang and started dating a man who'd lived in student co-op housing with us. They married and moved to Vancouver, where Samantha gave birth to a delightful little boy a couple of years before Astra was born. (Our hearts would be broken when he died suddenly of a heart attack in 2012.) By the time I came to Vancouver, Samantha and her husband had separated and she needed a housemate. It was perfect timing. After all that had happened to us years ago, here were Samantha and I, students again, living together with our children. Our relationship was strengthened as we helped and supported each other through many ordeals as full-time students and single moms.

I returned to Toronto when my daughter was four and was lucky to be accepted into the Bain Avenue housing co-op in Toronto's South Riverdale neighbourhood. Here, I joined committees and worked my way up to being elected president of the co-op. I learned Robert's Rules of Order, how to read financial statements, and how to negotiate and facilitate resolutions, and I found out that I was very good at these things.

I was hired as a receptionist at the local community health centre, a job I loved. Later I enrolled as a full-time student in a film and photography program at Ryerson University. Doing all of this—and doing it well—allowed me to develop a new self-confidence. On top of that, I fell in love and moved in with a wonderful man I met in the co-op. Doug became the best stepfather a child could ever have.

Now that I was back in Toronto, closer to Newfoundland and Labrador, and living a pretty settled life, I saw a lot more of my family. I had visited my parents in Labrador when Astra was a baby. She was a sweet little girl and I could tell they loved her immediately. My father was now retired and was able to move back "home," as he always referred to Newfoundland. He and my mother left Labrador and moved to Carbonear, around the bay from St. John's, where my sister

Edna lived with her husband, Jim, a doctor, and their two girls, Felicity and Virginia. We often went to visit them, and the three little cousins became very good friends.

Over time, my younger sister Joan had two children, Sonia and Charles, and my brother Max had three, J'Lynn, Laura, and Andrew. Joan and her family moved to Prince Rupert, British Columbia, when Sonia was still a baby. Charles was born there. We didn't get a chance to see them very much because they were so far away. But my parents would go to see them once a year, visit Max in Winnipeg for a couple of weeks, and then make their final stop in Toronto before heading home. Fred, the baby of the family, lived an adventurous life that took him all over the world. He ended up as a tour guide in Peru and finally settled down when he married a beautiful young woman from Lima. They now live in Victoria with their son, Nate.

After keeping my distance from my family after I left home, being back in touch felt great.

TEN

TO THE CORRIDORS OF POWER

W HEN ASTRA WAS nine years old, something unexpected happened. We were having a dinner party one night, and she was bored and generally making a nuisance of herself. At that age, she was beginning to show an interest in my life, and I had already recounted to her some sanitized versions of my hippie years and my travels in Europe and Africa. To keep her occupied, I gave her my old black sketchbook, which was full of drawings, I Ching readings, poems, and little stories. She happily took it upstairs.

Later that night, when the guests had left, she came downstairs looking very serious. She looked me straight in the eye and asked if it was true that she had a brother. She handed me a piece of paper.

Folded in the pages of the book I'd given her, she had found a copy of the first letter I'd sent to Family and Children's Services in Simcoe County asking for information that they were allowed by law to release—general information about the kind of home my son had gone to when he was adopted, but nothing that would identify him or the adoptive family. I had always planned to tell her when she got a little older, but this was way too soon.

Wanting to protect her, my first inclination was to lie, but she gave me a determined stare and demanded the truth. I told her the whole story, straight out. I was worried about how she would react, but I needn't have been. When Astra was five, she had sat in my lap, facing me eyeball-to-eyeball, and demanded, "Now wook, Mom, tell me the truth, is there a Santa Clause?" I started the usual utterances (well—lies) that we tell little children, but she picked up on my discomfort and, looking hard into my eyes, lisped, "Now wook, Mom, I want you to tell me the truth." So with great trepidation, I did.

Her response surprised me. Instead of showing disappointment, she smiled radiantly and threw her arms around me. "Oh, good," she said, "now I know it's you who gives me all the presents." That wasn't all. She pressed for more truth. "Is there an Easter Bunny? a tooth fairy?" I confessed to her that I hid the Easter eggs and put money under her pillow. She hugged me and went back to her five-year-old business. Now, just as she had been happy to know there was no Santa, she was overjoyed to learn that she had a big brother out there somewhere.

Through my work at the Bain Co-op, I got involved in local community issues. I co-founded an environmental organization in 1983 called Citizens for a Safe Environment and became a well-known environmental activist. Our group was formed to fight the City of Toronto's bid to build a large-scale garbage incinerator in our South Riverdale neighbourhood. There was already an old polluting incinerator in the area, as well as a number of industries, including a lead smelter, that had contaminated the area for years. Our city alderman, David Reville, got our group fifty thousand dollars in city funding (an enormous amount—we still don't know how he did it), so we could participate in environmental assessment hearings.

We hired expert witnesses and an excellent lawyer, David Starkman, and presented our case that the proposed new plant would

create more pollution in an already polluted area. To everyone's surprise, we won. We stopped the incinerator and, in the next several
years, we also succeeded in getting the notorious Commissioners
Street garbage incinerator shut down. I'm proud to say that Citizens
for a Safe Environment was also one of the first organizations to
petition city hall to bring in what is now known as the blue box
recycling system.

At the same time, I became an outspoken activist for affordable
housing, and an active parent at Withrow Public School, where my
daughter was a student. Through these activities, I developed a reputation as a strong spokesperson and advocate on many issues, and I was
frequently sought out by the media. I was often in contact with city
and provincial politicians, and saw first-hand how important it was
that community and environmental activists be elected.

The insecure little girl from Happy Valley was being replaced by
a confident, concerned mother who was ready to take on the world!

In 1988, I decided to run for Toronto city council against Fred
Beavis, an alderman who had served the ward for almost thirty years.
I ran as a feminist and environmentalist and hardly anyone—including pundits and the media—believed I could beat Beavis, a tough old
ward heeler, although I received powerful endorsements from *The
Globe and Mail* and the *Toronto Star*. On November 10, four days before
the election, I woke up to *The Globe and Mail*'s editorial headline:
"All we want for Christmas is to have Fred Beavis dislodged in Ward
8 by reform candidate Marilyn Churley." Against all predictions,
the editorialists got their wish. I won the seat handily.

On city council, I became close to Jack Layton, who, having been
elected in 1982, was already a veteran alderman. I had met Jack in the
early 1980s, while working on environmental and housing issues in
Riverdale. On council, Jack took me under his wing and I considered
myself lucky to have such a great mentor.

Running for city council, 1988.

Jack and I had a lot in common—we were both cyclists, for instance, and we cared about the same issues. Over the years, our friendship deepened and we shared the odd bottle of red wine. Jack would even play cupid and introduce me to Richard, with whom he had worked closely on the White Ribbon campaign to end violence against women. When we got married in 2009, Jack would proudly stand as Richard's best man.

Working with Jack and other like-minded people on council, I was able to champion many environmental causes. I also worked hard on women's equality issues. One of the first motions I put forward at city hall was one to change our title from *alderman* to *councillor*. The motion passed, despite bitter opposition from some of council's old

boys. I fought for equal prize money for females participating in cycling races in Toronto. They didn't get nearly the prize money the male racers got—the unfairness reminded me of my speaking contest experience as a girl, and I was having none of it.

Richard and me on our wedding day, June 2009, with my daughter, Astra, as maid of honour and Jack Layton as best man.

It's hard to fathom, but before my motion passed at a council meeting, I began getting death threats. It appeared that a few of those guys were afraid that phasing in equal prize money for women might cause the province to stop funding races altogether, and they wanted to scare me off.

I also brought the Energy Efficiency Office to city hall and continued to work with my community to get polluting industry out of our neighbourhood. I cut my political teeth at city hall and loved representing Riverdale, which was full of progressive people who were active in the community. But it didn't last long.

At the legislature as an MPP.

Two years later, Reville, then the MPP in my home riding of Riverdale (now called Toronto–Danforth), decided to retire. I was wooed by New Democratic Party leader Bob Rae to run provincially in Reville's place. I hadn't finished out my city council term and was quite reluctant to leave, but the polls indicated that the NDP would be lucky to hang onto its existing seats. Rae needed someone well known and well liked to run in the riding. I relented and took a leave of absence from city hall.

I'm glad I did. I got elected. In fact, I won all 103 polls in the riding—quite a remarkable feat. And the NDP, much to everyone's surprise, including our own, formed a majority government on September 6, 1990. Soon after the election, something incredible happened. I became the minister of consumer and commercial relations and the registrar general of Ontario. All of the province's birth and death records—including those of the son I'd given birth to in 1968—were under my watch.

I didn't know where my son was. I began dreaming up schemes to get staff to let me access and browse the files. For a while, it's all I thought about as I lay sleepless in my bed at night. But tempting as it was, I did not use my position of privilege to get at those files. I was desperate to find out what had happened to my son, and there were times when I think I could have thrown my scruples out the window.

I had one chance. The Government Services office that stored birth and death records had been moved to Thunder Bay by the Liberal government shortly before the 1990 election. As Ontario's new registrar general, I was part of the delegation that went to Thunder Bay to cut the ribbon at the official opening on June 14, 1991. My mind was in turmoil as I asked for a tour of where the records were kept. We were taken as a group to a vast room with what looked like millions of files.

I felt some of the frustration I had felt looking at my baby through the glass pane but not being able to get close to him. Somewhere in that very room were my son's birth and adoption records. But there just was no realistic way I could get at them. So close, yet still so far away. That's when I decided at last to begin actively looking for my son.

ELEVEN

A PUNITIVE POLICY

WHEN I BECAME a minister of the Ontario government, adoption disclosure reform was a controversial issue in the province. Grassroots organizations and academics who were lobbying for change represented thousands of adult adoptees seeking their basic human right to learn about their original identity, ethnicity, and medical history. Many mothers (and some fathers, too) wanted to know what had happened to their children, and many adoptive parents wanted their children to have access to their full biological histories. Working together, these groups would become a powerful force.

But there were those—including some very influential people—who lined up on the other side of the issue, opposing reform or disagreeing on what kind of reform should take place. Some opponents—often men of a certain age—feared that if the province gave adoptees full access to birth information, children who were previously unknown to them might show up on their doorsteps, perhaps making a financial claim on them. They also argued, though the argument was unfounded, that birth mothers had been promised confidentiality by the province.

Some adoptive parents feared that they might lose their children to the affections of newly found birth mothers. And a small group of adoptees felt that they should have full control over their personal information, including the right to deny their amended birth information to their biological parents.

In some ways, too, society clung to a long-held moral judgment of women who had had children out of wedlock. The issue of whether these mothers should know about the children they had given up was not high on the general public's list of human rights concerns. The moral judgment, after all, was the basis for the historical secrecy surrounding adoption of babies born outside of marriage, a secrecy that was founded in the social norms of the early twentieth century and that then became enshrined in law.

Until 1921 there had been no adoption law in Ontario. Private arrangements were made by contract, or people simply took children in to live with them. When Ontario's Adoption Act was passed in 1921, it did not seal the records. It wasn't until 1927 that the government created a closed adoption system, whereby babies adopted in Ontario were legally registered under the names of their new parents. Their original birth registration, along with any other information that might identify the biological family, was locked away in a secret file that could not be accessed by the adoptees, even as adults. Nor could the biological family have access to the child's new identifying information. This legislation reflected societal attitudes around the disgrace of having a baby out of wedlock, inheritance, legitimacy, and costs incurred by the government previous to the adoption. Until children were adopted, if they were, taxpayers were footing the bill. Karen Bridget Murray's paper "Governing Unwed Mothers in Toronto at the Turn of the Twentieth Century" (*Canadian Historical Review*, June 2004) gives some interesting insights into the prevailing mindset of the day.

Seemingly at odds with the broader societal push to promote the two-parent family, heterosexual family, adoptions by unmarried women were also allowed. Perhaps it was hoped that such adoptions would help rid Toronto streets of neglected children and obliterate baby farming, child abandonment, and infanticide, without need for institutional care. Whatever the rationale, the provision highlighted the maternalist sensibilities typical at the time and underscored the fact that it was primarily "improper" sexual conduct that rendered unwed mothers troublesome rather than the "single mother" family structures they formed.

Ample evidence indicates that unmarried mothers at this time were deliberately punished for being little sluts. In her 1998 book *"No Car, No Radio, No Liquor Permit": The Moral Regulation of Single Mothers in Ontario, 1920–1997,* Margaret Jane Hillyard Little wrote:

> The debate inside Queen's Park was only part of a larger controversy that continued concerning morality and premarital sex. Unwed mothers became the scapegoat for much of this societal turmoil about moral standards. Dr. Marion Hilliard, Chief of Obstetrics and Gynaecology at the Women's College Hospital (Toronto) believed that an unwed mother should be punished by having her child adopted.

Hillyard Little quotes Dr. Hilliard as saying, "When she renounces her child for its own good, the unwed mother has learned a lot. She has learned to pay the price of her misdemeanour, and this alone, if punishment is needed, is punishment enough." This opinion was stated in 1956 and came from one of the leading progressive health centres in this country.

A 1927 Report of the Super of Neglected and Dependent Children reads: "An important feature of the Adoption Act is that proceedings are private and confidential, as it is the invariable wish of foster parents that the child should not be handicapped in later life by the fact of adoption being broadcasted."

Why should we care about the attitudes of that time? Because even if they were not overtly stated, those attitudes continued to be reflected time and again as adoption activists and MPPS tried to reform adoption disclosure laws in Ontario.

From the time adoption secrecy was enshrined in the law in Ontario in 1927, no changes were made until 1979. Government records indicate that from 1921 to 1979, 250,000 children were adopted in Ontario. For many years, adoptees and their birth mothers suffered in silence.

The 1960s, though, brought changing moral values and, eventually, a lessening of the social stigma around adoption. In the 1970s, thousands of adoptees began to demand to know their biological roots. It took longer for mothers who had relinquished their babies to adoption to come forward, but they, too, slowly began to speak up about their experience and their need to know what had happened to their children.

Parent Finders was founded in Vancouver in 1974 by adoptee Joan Vanstone. The first Parent Finders chapter in Ontario was founded in Toronto in 1975 by Patricia Richardson. Shortly thereafter, Joan Marshall, along with a few friends, started the Ottawa Parent Finders group and Wendie Redmond founded a chapter in Hamilton. In 1977, with Mary Jane Brinkos serving as president, the Toronto group incorporated and became known as Parent Finders Inc. (PFI), and several satellite chapters began to form in the Toronto region. In 1979, while Judy Rice was serving as president of PFI, a large Parent Finders meeting was held in Toronto and the movement began to spread like wildfire. By the 1990s, there were active chapters all over the province.

Adoptees began to boldly speak out and pushed the Progressive Conservative government to hold the province's first public hearings on the issue. The hearings were completed in 1975, and the report commissioned by cabinet minister James Taylor published the following year recommended that adult adoptees be given full access to their personal birth information. Though the government chose not to act on that report, its recommendations gave Parent Finders and other advocates a huge boost and they kept the pressure on the provincial legislature.

Parent Finders had been lobbying hard for improved disclosure and in 1979, they had their first big victory when Ontario created North America's first adoption disclosure registry. This came about through the efforts of Ross McClellan, a Toronto New Democratic Party MPP. The Progressive Conservative government had introduced a child welfare bill that didn't contain any reforms to adoption disclosure. McClellan moved to amend the bill to create the adoption disclosure registry, meaning that Ontario would now lead the way on this issue.

Though an important step, this new registry provided only a passive system that required adult adoptees and birth parents both to register voluntarily. Through the Office of the Registrar General, copies of original birth registration and adoption orders were to be provided to an adult adoptee and the birth parent if each party consented that this information be opened to the other. If one party asked for information and the other party hadn't registered, then neither would get it. And once a match was made, both parties had to wait for non-identifying information about each other to be sent.

Another hitch was written into the legislation: if a match was made, adult adoptees had to either get written permission from their adoptive parents to proceed to a reunion or prove the adoptive parents were deceased and then get permission from the executor of the last surviving parent's will. McClellan told me that he reluctantly went along with this provision in order to give his amendment a chance to pass.

Even with this power given to adoptive parents over their adult children, McClellan's amendment met ferocious opposition from the governing Progressive Conservatives. During the debate on the amendment, they were hostile toward any move that might disrupt adoptive parents' lives. They didn't demonstrate any concern about adult adoptees' need to know their biological history and birth mothers' desire to know what had happened to their children. It looked like the amendment would be defeated, until one of McClellan's colleagues, Evelyn Gigantes, a passionate and articulate supporter of adoption disclosure reform and an adoptive parent herself, read a note from a woman who was looking for her biological mother. The note said, in part:

I've looked in nursing homes and obit columns for my mother's name. For more than thirty years I've asked my government for help because every day of my life I think about my mother and pray that one day I will stand before the woman who gave me life to let her know that I am worth the pain or shame or whatever she felt for my existence. I have to believe she wants that satisfaction. I believe I have that right.

The woman who wrote that note, Mary Keenan, was sitting in the public gallery. In her 2000 book *Molly: Child Number 583*, she describes the electric moment when Gigantes, acknowledging her with a slight nod of her head, read her letter. Keenan describes a stunned hush after the note was read; it appears to have changed enough minds to allow the amendment to pass by one vote.

In 1980 Frank Drea, the minister of community and social services, attempted to set the clock back by amending the Child Welfare Act to prevent adoptees from gaining any access to birth information, including their medical histories and other non-identifying information. Thankfully, there was such an outcry that he was forced to back off.

The community of people opposing adoption secrecy continued to grow, and in 1982 the courts were brought into the debate. In a well-known case brought by a director of Parent Finders, Elizabeth Ferguson argued that her file should be opened on the grounds that, as an adult adoptee, she could show she had "good cause" to be granted her personal information. However, Justice Gordon Killeen ruled that there was no mechanism in law to either grant or deny her request.

As a result of Justice Killeen's decision in the *Ferguson* case and the outrage in the adoption community over Drea's regressive proposals, the new Progressive Conservative minister of community and social services, Robert Elgie, commissioned Ralph Garber to conduct an inquiry into adoption disclosure. Dr. Garber's report was released in November 1985, after extensive research, input from experts and the adoption community, and examination of disclosure policies in other jurisdictions. The report recommended that adult adoptees have unqualified access to their personal birth information and that birth families have access, with consent, to identifying information about the adult adoptee.

Garber acknowledged that the system had historically been unfair, and he stated that the changes he was proposing were "meant to redress the wrongs or limitations imposed upon birth parents, adoptees, and adoptive parents by previous legislation."

Regrettably, Garber's major recommendations, like those of the Taylor Report, were shelved. But both reports proved to be important to the reform movement as it expanded and pushed even harder for change. Taylor and Garber are well regarded in the adoption community for their early groundbreaking work.

Parent Finders, encouraged by Garber's recommendations, began to have some successes, and in 1987, John Sweeney, minister of community and social services in the new Liberal government, made crucial reforms to the Child and Family Services Act. Although the Garber recommendation that records be made available upon request to adult adoptees was not followed, the government took away adoptive parents' right to veto adult adoptees from reuniting with their birth parents. As well, Sweeney amended the adoption disclosure registry provisions to allow the registrar general to conduct searches on behalf of adult adoptees to find out whether their birth parents wanted to reunite with them. Non-identifying information was defined and codified, and for the first time, birth parents could apply to the Children's Aid Society and receive this information about their adult children. (Adoptees were already allowed to access non-identifying information.)

Unfortunately the government also saw fit to bring in mandatory counselling at this time. The stated purpose of the counselling was to ensure that people were emotionally prepared to deal with the impact that a possible reunion might have. However, its mandatory nature ignored the fact that these people were adults who may well already have come to terms with the possibility of reunion, some through counselling on their own, and others—like me—without it.

But the restrictions on full access to birth records to adoptees and their birth parents remained. If just one of the parties signed up for the optional registry or if one of them quit during the long process, the other party was out of luck and was denied access to the information. So few staff were assigned to matching requests to the registry that over time, a stunning backlog of up to twelve years built up before people could get their original birth information. The government was also supposed to conduct a search on behalf of a person who needed to pass on information about life-threatening diseases, but all too often, even this was not done.

That's where things stood when I was first elected to the Ontario government in 1990, and began, reluctantly at first, to enter the fray.

TWELVE

THE DAY ARRIVES

N JANUARY 1994, just a few months after Bob Rae sought my support, as registrar general, of Tony Martin's Bill 158, I got a lead about my son's whereabouts. Back in the mid-1980s I had applied to the Family and Children's Services office in Simcoe County for non-identifying information about the people who had adopted my son—things about them and the circumstances of the adoption, but not anything that would positively identify them. It was a copy of this letter that my daughter Astra had confronted me with. In April 1985, the office sent me a patronizing note telling me that I, as the birth mother, was not entitled to that information. But I kept trying, and almost a decade later, I received the information I had requested.

All along, I'd known my son's birth date, obviously. I'd also known the date and region in which the adoption had taken place; at the time, papers had been sent to me to sign. Now I learned that his parents were involved in a local Dutch church and that at the time of adoption they owned a small fabric business.

I had always intended to look for my son someday, but I'd hoped that he would take the initiative and find me. I made it as easy as possible to locate me should he begin a search. Churley is an unusual name, and mine was the only listing with that spelling in Toronto's huge phone book.

In 1985, I had also filed with Ontario's adoption registry, but they informed me after a few years that, since my son had not registered, they were unable to proceed. At about the same time I registered with Parent Finders, the oldest and largest organization for members of the adoption community in Canada. They had years of experience and information about adoption, search, and reunion. I received their monthly newsletters, and for years I would eagerly scan the list of adoptees searching for their birth mothers. And each month I would be disappointed.

Now that I had more to go on, you might think that I would become more active in my search right away. But I didn't know where to begin, and as much as I wanted to find my son, I still hoped that he would contact me first; that way, there would be no risk of my barging into his life and being turned away. I just sat on the information for a while. When I did decide in 1995 to start a search, it occurred to me just whom to call for help—Holly Kramer, then president of Parent Finders Inc. Holly and I worked together on Tony Martin's adoption disclosure bill, and she told me that in the 1970s, on her own initiative, she had found her birth mother.

Holly was a shrewd leader, articulate and smart as a whip. Her sparkling blue eyes positively crackled with purpose and clarity. She was the go-to person for the media and politicians alike when they wanted information on adoption disclosure, and she knew all about lobbying the government. Holly never referred to adult adoptees as adopted "children," and it really irritated her when other people did. She wanted to be sure that politicians and the public knew we were talking about the rights of adults, not children, to gain access to their histories. And I knew that Holly was very generous with her expertise and with her time in helping people search for each other.

Using the little information I had about my son's adoptive parents, Holly began conducting a search on my behalf. I didn't have much, but Holly said I was lucky compared to many others who were doing the same kind of thing.

Holly enlisted the help of Alice MacDonald, a pioneer in adoption reunions long before computer databases were created. Alice and her

The woman who found my son: Holly Kramer, former president of Parent Finders Inc.

husband, Rick, scoured old newspapers for adoption notices. Then, in a spreadsheet, they entered the names in alphabetical order, along with all the accompanying information. Adoption notices typically gave the baby's approximate date of birth; names of adoptive parents, grandparents, and siblings; the adoptive mother's birth name and place of residence—in short, quite a bit of information. Eventually, Alice and Rick started the Canadian Adoptees Registry Inc. (CARI). Working as a full-time volunteer, Alice was responsible for bringing many families together.

With my information in hand, Holly asked Alice to look at her list of notices in that time frame and area. The pair started checking old city directories, looking for men's occupations. Eventually they hit upon a family that was connected to a fabric store and had a Dutch-sounding name, and they were able to learn the names of everyone in that family. We were off and running.

Holly used whatever secret methods she had at her disposal. Running the name through Canada 411, which at the time was published quarterly on diskette, she discovered that the family lived not too far away from where they'd been in the late 1960s and early '70s. Holly and Alice believed that the family's son William could be the child I was looking for. They were able to find out where the children from that family went to school. It turned out that Alice's daughter had gone to the same high school in the early 1980s, so Alice asked her whether she was aware that the boy she had known as William was adopted, and whether she knew if William knew it. The answer was yes to both questions. After a bit more sleuthing, they confirmed that his date of birth was the same as that of the son I had named Andrew, and they began searching for the family's address.

Alice, whom I hadn't met, kindly mailed me a blurry black-and-white photocopy of William's picture from his high school yearbook. Though I couldn't quite make out his features, it was still the first glimpse I had of my son in almost thirty years. (Alice would die suddenly in 2010, but her invaluable work still lives on. Gail Hadley and a few other dedicated volunteers continue to maintain the CARI database and give hope to thousands of people like me; the site is "dedicated to the memory of our angel, Alice.")

The process of searching for my son took more than a year. During that year, Mike Harris's Progressive Conservatives won a majority government. Premier Bob Rae and the NDP, buffeted by a difficult term in office that coincided with a serious worldwide recession, were thrown out of power. I now found myself sitting with only sixteen fellow New Democrats on the opposition benches.

Then one night in November 1995, I came home to a telephone message from Holly. She had some information. I was trembling when I picked up the phone to call her back. The news was good— Holly had found my son's adoptive family, and although she was unable to locate him directly, she had the name and address of his brother.

This she knew for certain: the son I had named Andrew had been renamed William. I had his full name, and I had an address through which he could be reached.

My reaction was intense. I put down the phone feeling completely overwhelmed. I started to tremble uncontrollably. What felt like a tight spring in the pit of my stomach—something that had likely been there for years—began to uncoil in waves, and finally I felt it melt away.

My son's name is William. My son's name is William. My son's name is William.

I finally had a little piece of him. It was so precious that I wrote it down, put it in an envelope, and carried it with me everywhere. I often would slip it out and stare at it, and at night I kept it under my pillow. *My son's name is William.*

I decided to write him a letter and send it to his brother's address, the only address I had. What do you say to your child who is not your child, to someone you love but don't know at all, to someone you are not sure will welcome a letter from you?

I sat on my bed with a pad of paper, struggling to find the words. I wasn't certain he knew that he was adopted, but I had to proceed on the assumption that he did. Working determinedly, I ripped up page after page of rejected attempts. Finally, I decided to keep it simple, and mention only a few key things: I didn't want to cause any upheaval in his life. It was his decision whether we should meet. He had a half-sister who was dying to meet him. And at the very least, no matter what he decided to do, I longed for him to send me a picture so I'd know what he looked like.

I mailed my letter on November 29, 1995, with a covering letter from Holly written in the careful terms that such letters use. Here is what she wrote:

29.11.1995

TO BE OPENED ONLY BY ADDRESSEE

PRIVATE AND STRICTLY CONFIDENTIAL

Dear Mr. Boertjes,

I am writing to you on behalf of my friend, Marilyn, about a very personal matter. I've sent this letter in care of your brother Brian, because I was unable to determine your personal mailing address through public records, and unwilling to disclose the reason for my wanting to get in touch with you to anyone else.

When she was very young, Marilyn gave a child to adoption. The social climate at that time left her little alternative, as she was single and unable to care for him by herself. She wanted her son to have all of the benefits of the love of two mature parents, financial security and a stable home. She hoped that he be nurtured and cared for, at least as much as she loved and cared for him.

Marilyn's son was born on January 30th, 1968 in Barrie, and she named him Andrew. On February 9th, he went home to his parents and his named was changed to William.

Since then, not a day has gone by that Marilyn hasn't thought of her birth son, worried and wondered whether he is alive and well and happy. Some time ago she registered with the provincial disclosure registry; however, due to funding cutbacks and a lengthy waiting list for services, about a year ago, we began to conduct a discreet, active search using the non-identifying information supplied under Ontario's Child & Family Services Act, old city directories and the like.

I too was adopted. I found my birth mother in 1979 through my own efforts, and for us reunion has been a joyous experience and one which I wish all adopted people and their birth mothers could share. I was fortunate in that I had the support of my family. Though some people choose—understandably—to keep contact with a birth relative very private, in the sixteen years I have worked in this field more often than not adoptees are delightfully surprised to learn that their parents want to share this with them.

In any case, Marilyn has no desire to disrupt anyone's lives. She would like very much to correspond with her birth son, and to meet him, even once. She needs to know that he is okay, that he understands why she had to relinquish him, and to reassure herself that she made the right decision under the circumstances.

Never the less, Marilyn will respect his feelings and wishes: she sincerely has no intention of intruding.

I'd like to add here that Marilyn is a lovely woman—kind, empathetic, bright, with a wonderful sense of humour and a demonstrated social conscience. She is well educated, holds a respected position, and is well thought of by her colleagues, many friends and in her community.

I truly hope that you will be able to help Marilyn complete her search and that you will find it in your heart to get in touch with one of us. Enclosed is a sealed note from Marilyn and a self-addressed envelope. If you would rather talk, don't hesitate to call (collect) in confidence.

Thank you very much for your consideration.

Yours sincerely

Holly Kramer

I followed Parent Finders' recommended process for making that first contact: the return address and phone number were in care of Holly at Parent Finders. Now all I could do was wait. It was one of the hardest things I've ever had to do.

Christmas came and went. Nothing. Even though I knew I shouldn't, I had built up my hope that I would be sharing that Christmas with my son and my daughter together.

In January 1996, Holly called. I could hear the excitement in her voice. She'd heard from William.

It took a few minutes for this news to kick in. Then I asked her a million questions: What was his voice like? What did he do? Was he married? Did he sound kind? Did he seem hostile? Did he want to meet me? She laughed and patiently told me that he was a university student, that he wanted me to know that he harboured no hard feelings toward me, and that he would be writing to me soon.

It was another agonizing wait. February passed. Then came March, with the legislature recessed for a week during spring break. On Tuesday, March 12, a lovely spring day, I finished a mountain of constituency work and went to a movie with my friend Lesley. When I got home, I reached into the mailbox. I was used to coming out disappointed, but on that day, there it was—a letter with William's name and return address.

I went inside and sat on the couch, studying the unusually beautiful handwriting on the envelope. Then, slowly, I opened it. The letter was very kind, beginning with an apology for the delay in his response. He explained that he was attending university in Waterloo and his brother had called him to tell him a registered letter had arrived from someone named Holly Kramer. He didn't have a clue who Holly was, so he was not particularly concerned, and he asked his brother to just hold onto it until he came home for Christmas.

William wrote that while visiting his family on Christmas Eve, he had opened the letter and had been stunned by its contents. He did not tell his family immediately, but took the letter back with him to Waterloo. He needed some time to digest it and decide what to do. He said that he was shocked to hear from me, but that he had always known he was adopted, that he had often wondered about me and didn't resent me or hate me. He said his adoptive parents were the

This is the photo Billy sent in his first letter—my first glimpse of my son's face since I said goodbye in 1968.

kindest people in the world; they loved him unconditionally and would do anything for him. He wanted us to correspond for a while, to get to know more about each other before we met.

Folded in the letter was a beautiful colour photograph. He was wearing a tux, walking down the aisle at his brother's wedding. He was slender, with dark hair down to his shoulders, and he was absolutely gorgeous. Like Brad Pitt, only better. I carried that picture everywhere and kept it in front of me, no matter what I was doing. I even propped it up on my water glass at my legislature desk and stared at it between questions.

I couldn't get enough of that face—my son's face, more than twenty-eight years later.

We sent letters and pictures back and forth, telling each other about our lives, about our families, about our likes and dislikes. I had kept my daughter, who was twenty-two years old and a new young mother herself, in the loop throughout all of this. Now I hightailed it to her house to show her that first letter. She was as excited as I was and couldn't wait to see him.

I wrote back immediately and, after we'd exchanged a few letters, I started to think that if I didn't make a move soon, our meeting might never happen. He had mentioned in his second letter to me that he felt ready, but he had exams the week of April 22 so it would have to be after that. Then there was silence. It was making me crazy. I was dying to see my son, to touch him and to hug him if he'd let me.

I fantasized about driving to Waterloo and parking outside his unit just to get a look at him. I wouldn't do anything to alienate him or make him hesitate to see me, but I was getting impatient. My first letter to him had been sent in January, and we still had not met or spoken on the phone.

One chilly evening in early May, I had a meeting in my constituency with Jack Layton, who was then the city councillor in my riding. Jack had been there through every step of my search for my son. That evening, we went out to a bar and I told him how frustrating it was waiting for my son to suggest a time to meet. Jack replied, with a twinkle in his eye, that if William was like most guys, it might take him a while to get in touch. He suggested that I take the bull by the horns and try to set something up.

I came home just tipsy enough to muster some courage, strode purposefully into the house and, without taking off my hat or gloves, picked up the phone and dialled 411. I had no idea if William had a phone listed under his name—he was sharing a townhouse with other students—but I gave his name to the operator and got a number. I punched it in.

The phone rang. A male voice said, "Hello."

"Is William there, please?"

"Speaking."

My knees buckled. This was the first time I had heard his voice. "William, this is Marilyn," I said calmly, though shaking on the inside. "I don't know about you, but I think it's time we set a date to get together."

I held my breath. There was a long hesitation. Then he said yes, he was ready, too. We set it up for the following week.

I dressed carefully that day, like I was going on a first date. I was so excited in the car that just before I got on the highway, I spilled coffee all over myself and had to go home and change. When I got to Waterloo, already forty-five minutes late, I promptly got lost. I pulled over and called his number from a pay phone. It turned out I was only five minutes from his door. The moment I had waited so long for was about to happen.

I was trembling as I approached the door. It was an ordinary door, but I knew that when it opened, I would enter an extraordinary new world. I had spent so many years thinking about the day when I would come face to face with my son. But now that it was here, I was barely thinking at all. I could feel my heart racing and my body trembling; my mind went very, very still. I was simply in the moment.

I knocked. Waited. Heard footsteps.

The door opened and there he was—my son.

We stood there transfixed. The world around me disappeared. It was just him and me, inches apart. The last time I had seen him was the heartbreaking day I said goodbye through a pane of glass, telling him that I would find him some day. And the day had arrived.

Eventually the world righted itself and the ordinary neighbourhood sounds of chirping birds and cars whizzing by filled my ears. We stood in the open doorway intensely taking each other in; I didn't know what I should do next.

Then he held out his arms to me. And I knew everything was going to be all right. We hugged for a long time and we cried. It was the first time I had ever held my son in my arms.

With Billy in the early days of our reunion.

"Hello, William," I finally said.

"I'm called Bill," he answered.

"Hello, Billy."

We talked for hours. He wanted to know everything about his birth. I was so happy that I went on and on, telling him far too much about what had happened between his father and me. I told him that I always looked for him on street corners and that each year I lit a candle on his birthday. I told him how my heart had ached for him and that I knew I could never be at peace until I found him.

And he told me all about his life. He said he'd always known my last name because it was on the adoption order given to his adoptive parents. He'd seen my signature on safety certificates in elevators in the early part of the decade, when I was the minister of consumer and commercial relations. Churley is not a common name, and he did wonder from time to time if I could be his mother. But then he'd think, "Naw, I couldn't possibly have a mother whose signature was in every elevator in Ontario!"

I always blew out candles for my son on his birthday. Here he is at two years old.

I drove to Waterloo as often as possible to visit Billy. Astra and I went to his twenty-ninth birthday party. I had marked his birthdays every year by going into a room alone, lighting and blowing out a candle, and making a wish for my son. And every year I would shed bitter tears. This year I was going to share that moment with him for the first time.

The house was full of boisterous university students, the music was loud, and the party was in full swing, but late in the evening, I caught his eye and without any words, we went into his room and closed the door. I held a beautiful white scented candle in both my hands as Billy lit it. We looked into each other's eyes, made silent wishes, whispered *one, two, three,* and together blew out the candle. I wished him happy birthday and we hugged each other tight. This time the tears I shed were tears of joy.

PART III

FIVE TIMES TO THE BRINK

THIRTEEN

OUT OF THE CLOSET

FOR THE LONGEST TIME, I kept a distance from the issues surrounding adoption and information disclosure. In 1993, when the premier asked me to help with Tony Martin's private member's bill, I had frozen at the mere thought of it. Rather than take on an emotional attachment to the cause, I kept busy with all the other things that a minister with an active, engaged constituency in a government under siege would be kept busy with. At that point, I just did what I had to do as registrar general to help with the drafting of the legislation.

Only after I publicly revealed my first-hand experience did I realize how little I'd dealt with my emotions, emotions that linger long after a woman relinquishes a child to adoption. I went public with my story in 1997. My parents didn't know about Billy's existence, and I hadn't yet spoken to Billy's adoptive parents, although they were aware that we had connected. But news broke about Canadian folk icon Joni Mitchell's reunion with the daughter she had given up for adoption in 1965, and that essentially forced me out of the closet.

My revelation took place just as we—the seventeen New Democrats who were left standing after Harris won a Progressive Conservative majority two years earlier—staged a filibuster in the legislature to protest the controversial bill to amalgamate the City of Toronto and the municipalities of York, East York, North York, Etobicoke, and Scarborough. The NDP had been hounded by critics incessantly and blamed for just about every possible problem, but while Harris campaigned on a promise to tear up most of the programs initiated by the New Democrats, his platform didn't mention anything about amalgamation. When the bill was introduced, people were up in arms. They identified with their municipalities and their local services, and they were very upset over this bid to bring them together under one government. The government barged ahead despite large organized protests led by former mayor John Sewell and other community activists, including Kathleen Wynne, who was then a school trustee and is now premier of Ontario.

At Queen's Park, the opposition New Democrats and Liberals sought ways to slow down the legislation to allow public pressure on the Harris government to build. Frances Lankin, our party whip, discovered a cunning way to do that within the legislative rules. Every street in the five municipalities was named in the legislation in one long clause—12,500 street names listed on thousands of pages. Under the rules of the legislature, we were able to compel the government to read every street name into the record and force a standing vote on each one that had to be counted and recorded.

Because these amendments were sent to the Committee of the Whole House, they had to be dealt with in the legislative chamber instead of a committee room, in order to give every member an opportunity to participate. On a motion by the government, the committee was to stay in session around the clock until every last street was counted and recorded. As a result, for nine days running, the regular business of the legislature—such as question period and introduction and debate of bills and petitions—came to a dramatic and abrupt end as street names were read in and voted on one by one.

I was one of three committee chairs who presided. We each assumed our position at the head of the table for two hours, then rested for four. I brought in bedding, extra clothes, and toiletries, and set up camp in my office.

In October 1997, I was appointed deputy Speaker in the Ontario legislature.

Because there was so much opposition to the bill, the nine-day filibuster became the most-watched show in Toronto, with many viewers tuning in to the legislature channel in the middle of the night. People brought in food and sent flowers at all hours of the day and night, and when my voice started to go, they sent lozenges. I even received a message from a doctor who was watching at three in the morning as I struggled to talk with a hoarse voice. He noticed I was drinking ice water and phoned to tell me that hot water would help my throat. From then on, the attendants kept a kettle on and brought me hot water all night long. It worked.

In the middle of this kerfuffle, the story about Joni Mitchell and her reunion with her daughter broke. An article by Michael Hanlon appeared in the *Toronto Star* on April 10 headed "Adopting Joni's child created 'a nightmare': Couple always feared losing their daughter." The story stated that the couple also expressed concern about others taking the same step. "They wonder if the publicity this particular mother-and-child reunion has garnered will streamline the system and somehow make it easier for adopted children and birth parents to find each other."

I was alarmed when I read that story, and so were many advocates for open adoption records. We were in the process of preparing my first private member's bill to reform adoption disclosure in Ontario, Bill 88. This story had the potential to cause a backlash against opening up the records. Our position had to be articulated quickly, and leaders in the adoption community felt that I was in the best position to do it. It was time to publicly reveal my personal experience with adoption.

So at two in the morning, bleary-eyed and weeping silently, I sat in my office and wrote about the birth of my son, the adoption, and the subsequent reunion. I finished a first draft and then went down to the legislature to continue my duties for another two hours. When I got back to my office, I called *Toronto Star* columnist Ian Urquhart to ask if the *Star* might be interested in publishing my story. With his help, my op-ed piece was published in the paper a few days later, accompanied by a photo of me and my son. It appeared under the headline "After 29 Years, a Loving Circle Is Complete."

In the piece, I recounted the trauma of being a pregnant teenager in 1968, of giving birth and having my son taken from me. I described the joy—the utter joy—of my reunion with Billy. And then I addressed the concerns of adoptive parents:

I would say this to loving adoptive parents: Please know that finding a birth mother does not mean you are losing your child. It is clear that Bill's mum is his mum—he loves her in a way that he will never love me. And I don't expect him to. We have a different relationship from mother and son, one that is hard to describe because it is unlike any other relationship I've had. I believe every human being should have the right to know their biological history, and Billy now knows where he comes from. . . . He knows now he wasn't abandoned, but reluctantly relinquished in great sorrow and love. I haven't met his parents yet, but I will soon. Billy loves them very much.

I want them to know how grateful I am that Billy has such loving, wonderful parents. And I want them to know that because he has been brought into the loving circle of my family, this in no way diminishes the love and deep connection he has to them. . . . They are his parents and nobody can take that away. But I am the woman who nurtured him inside my body and brought him into the world; this also cannot be changed.

After this story was published, everything changed for me and for the adoption community. I was asked to do many TV and radio interviews. Billy and I were guests on the popular Jane Hawtin talk show. Several supportive newspaper articles were written, including a lovely piece by Alison Uncles of the *Ottawa Citizen* entitled "MPP proudly reveals secret."

I was now well positioned to influence public opinion and help change the laws. People told me I brought a bourgeois respectability to the movement, which made me laugh, but I guess it was true. I was a high-profile MPP who came out of the closet, and my revelation began to shift the perception of what unwed mothers who relinquished their children to adoption looked like.

Nonetheless, I was stunned to receive hundreds of letters and emails from all over the world. The vast majority were supportive, but I did get a few nasty ones, like the memorable message that said: "You little slut—you had your fun and what gives you the right to your son?" Those I threw in the garbage.

My unashamed revelation opened up the floodgates. I heard from grown adoptees who were sick of being treated like children, who asked for my help to change the laws so they could get access to their own birth information. Desperate mothers pleaded with me to help them find their lost children. The longing in those handwritten letters was palpable. Those from elderly women were particularly moving; they described having suffered their entire adult lives wondering what happened to their children, and wanting to know before they died. I couldn't stand the thought of being their age and never having learned what happened to my son. Many letters came from adoptive parents who wanted to help their children find their birth mothers, and from adoptees who were starting their own families and were urgently seeking health information about their biological families.

Members of the volunteer organizations were overjoyed by the enormous attention my story was receiving, and they wrote me letters to express their appreciation. Holly Kramer, president of Parent Finders Inc., wrote: "On behalf of Ontario's adoption community: thank you Marilyn! Our thanks too, to Bill for 'standing up to be counted,' and helping to de-mystify and normalize our mutual cause!"

Patricia McCarron, president of the National Capital Region of Parent Finders, who had long been involved in the struggle to reform adoption disclosure laws, wrote: "Dear Ms Churley, The Board of Directors of Parent Finders National Capital Region would like to congratulate you on a successful reunion with your son. You are to be commended for sharing your story publicly and may not realize the positive impact this has on members of organizations such as ours."

Because I was a well-known politician, I knew that the media would pick up my story and it would be all over the country as soon as it was published. I'd tried to think through the implications. Billy's adoptive parents knew that we had connected, but we had not spoken, so I got Billy to arrange a time for us to talk before publication. I didn't know how they'd respond, and I was worried they'd be upset about it.

When I explained, talking to the couple on speakerphone, why I had decided to tell my story in a newspaper, I was relieved that they seemed to take it in stride. With that out of the way, we talked for a while about Billy and the new realities for both our families. As we ended the conversation, Billy's father, Bram, his voice breaking, said, "Marilyn, we always considered you a part of the family. After all, without your great sacrifice we never would have had our son. Thank you." Billy's mother, Helen, chimed in with her agreement.

It was an emotional moment for all of us, and one we have built on. When Bram and Helen came to Toronto to meet me shortly after the article was published, we were shy with each other at first. We all piled into their car and went out to lunch with Billy. It didn't take long for our curiosity about each other to emerge. They told me about their other two adopted children, and I told them about my family. I must have asked a million questions about what Billy was like growing up. And they were happy to oblige me.

Bram and Helen and I now see each other quite frequently, because we share a little grandson. Tristan was born on December 23, 2009, and his parents throw birthday parties for him at their house. At one of those parties, I was sitting next to Helen, and a friend of Billy's wife, Milena, came over to introduce him. Helen smiled politely and said, "Nice to meet you. I'm Helen and this is Marilyn. We're Billy's two moms."

The fellow looked a little confused, then seemed to understand and after a few minutes of conversation, he moved on. I thanked Helen for acknowledging me, but then mentioned the implications of describing us as his two mothers. She turned beet red and we had a good laugh.

As for my parents, I couldn't risk letting them find out inadvertently. They happened to be visiting my brother Max and his family in Winnipeg when my story was publicized, and he and his wife, Joan, were put to the task of keeping them from watching the news that day. This was no small thing because my father was a serious news junkie. But somehow they did it.

From the day my article was published, I was approached by women—often strangers or colleagues at work, but sometimes women I had known for years—who told me that they, too, had relinquished a child to adoption. Some had never told another soul. Some were searching and wanted help. One day, walking in my neighbourhood, I was alarmed when an old friend approached me with slow, tentative steps. She usually walked with grace and confidence, so I could tell something was wrong. With tears streaming, she told me she had relinquished a baby girl to adoption and, to cope with the trauma, had put that whole time of her life out of mind. She said that my story had made her think about that daughter again.

"Why don't you begin a search?" I suggested. "I'll help you."

"I didn't keep any of the documents," she wailed. "And I don't remember the exact date of her birth."

I was flabbergasted; this was the first time I had met a birth mother who had forgotten the date of her child's birth. But I have since discovered that some young women were so traumatized that the only way they could deal with it was to put the incident out of their minds. Not that they forgot that they gave birth to a child. How could a woman forget a thing like that?

Of course, my friend hadn't forgotten, and her story would have a happy ending. When I ran into her recently, she approached me with sparkling eyes and a huge grin. Whispering "Come here, I have something to tell you," she drew me aside and told me that she had recently come home to a registered letter from her daughter and they had since had a joyful reunion. She was glowing with happiness.

After my article appeared, I started to understand that I, too, had harboured a kind of shame that didn't exactly have to do with having a child out of wedlock. What I had felt ashamed of was my sorrow and longing for the child I had lost. I thought I would be seen as self-indulgent and emotionally unstable if I ever revealed how I felt. So I'd kept it to myself.

Really, my feelings were the outcome of a system that was set up to discourage mothers from dealing openly with what they had gone through. The entire process—from pregnancy to delivery to adoption—was shrouded in secrecy and shame, both of which were bound to take an emotional toll. I was told that lots of young women like me had given up their babies, then forgot about it and got on with their lives—kind of like having your tonsils removed. I was brainwashed into believing that it was unnatural to feel the way I did.

But the system kept it all a secret. You were a bad girl and you were treated accordingly. Canadian journalist Anne Petrie, in her 1998 book *Gone to an Aunt's*, tells her story and those of six other women who were sent to homes for unwed mothers until their babies were born. She writes about why she and the others were compelled to hide out:

> You knew, or thought you knew, all too well how your parents would react. It would be easier to say you murdered someone; at least you might have the defence of age. But not for this—this was the great crime of youth, especially for a girl. It meant you had sex "out of wedlock", and now everyone will know. You are a slut. Pure and

simple. There was no other explanation. Your parents would kill you or at least disown you.

Ann Fessler, in an interview with Salon.com shortly after her 2006 book *The Girls Who Went Away* was published, said:

> Secrecy was imperative. There was no reason to send a woman away and give up a child if you weren't going to keep it quiet; the idea was that no one would ever know. That was what the families wanted and in some cases the women, too—they knew what the social stigma was like, and they just felt like they could not deal with it. They knew what the image of an unwed mother was. And it wasn't them.

Fessler went on to talk about how damaging the burden of maintaining a lie can be and how much women suffer from an ongoing sense of worry about their children. She said that some studies equated it with having a loved one missing in action.

From 1974, when I gave birth to my daughter, to 1996, when I found my son, when people asked me how many children I had, I would politely answer "one." But inside, I was crying, "Two! I have *two* children!" Having a baby and giving it up for adoption was just not talked about in polite company. If I did talk about it, I felt people would judge me harshly or feel sorry for me, but not give me what I really wanted—the acknowledgement that I did have two children, one as dear to me as the other. My inner voice was always saying, *He isn't really your son—he's somebody else's. You voluntarily gave him away. Don't bring it up.*

When I was pulling materials together to write this book, I came across a batch of yellowing sheets covered with tiny handwriting about my trip to Europe and North Africa in 1970. I read through the accounts, alone at the cottage with candles glowing and wine flowing. I laughed and cried; I remembered events and people long forgotten. I was pleased with my own descriptions and insights. But what astounded me was that I had written almost nothing about the chunk of me that was missing.

The only time I mentioned my baby was in recounting a deeply hurtful incident that took place in Luxembourg. I was hanging out with a group of young people I had just met, exchanging stories and travel adventures. Sparks were flying between me and a good-looking guy who was sitting next to me on the floor. While we sat and made eyes at each other, one of the young men began talking about his little boy back in the United States and how much he missed him— and I couldn't help myself. I saw an opening and jumped in. I told them that I, too, had a little boy at home with my husband and that I missed him terribly. I dared not tell them the truth about the adoption; I was craving the same sympathy and kindness so generously given to the young father, and I was sure they would not be able to relate to my true situation. But my revelation backfired horribly. They all looked at me like I was some kind of hideous creature and the guy who was flirting with me now looked at me in revulsion, asking harshly what kind of mother I was to leave my child behind. Then he left the room.

Hey! Yoo-hoo! There was a dad there travelling the planet for months who had left his baby behind. That same old double standard.

Other than that little entry, you would think I had moved on and forgotten all about it, but I know I thought about him every single day. Why didn't I write down those thoughts of my baby?

After my story was published, I heard from many birth mothers who told me they had experienced similar feelings, and I was relieved to find out that mine were typical after all. I'm so grateful to have met these women and thankful for the gift they gave me—the gift of understanding that the intense emotions around the loss of my child were normal. This knowledge allowed a fierce passion to blossom inside me, a passion I poured into fighting openly and proudly for justice for biological parents and adoptees.

That gift came with a big price tag, though. On many an occasion, I angered colleagues as I fought to get adoption bills though the legislature. I'd get into nasty fights with some of my NDP colleagues and particularly with Peter Kormos, who was our house leader throughout most of my adoption disclosure battles. He was a quirky, brilliant parliamentarian who knew his way around the rules of order and liked to stir things up. Kormos would die suddenly in March 2013.

Some members with competing interests felt I was standing in the way of getting their bills passed. The real struggle would come as the three party house leaders huddled in private to determine which bills would be allowed to pass in the limited time before the end of the session. I always insisted my adoption bills be on our priority list, and that inevitably led to trouble.

I know that my outspokenness, my stubbornness, my self-righteousness and quick temper (which, my family will attest, I come by honestly), my determination to do the right thing, and my hatred of duplicity were my biggest strengths. But they could also be my biggest weaknesses as a politician. Those qualities made me a strong advocate and an effective troublemaker on many issues. I fearlessly stood up against the status quo and for the rights of the disenfranchised. Many voters across the political spectrum supported me because of those qualities. They respected my integrity even if they didn't always agree with me, and they knew I would fight tooth and nail for them.

When I got into the fight for the rights of adoptees and their birth mothers, I was willing to walk over hot coals. And sometimes, it felt like I was.

FOURTEEN

HANGING OUT WITH BILLY

FOR A MOTHER who had relinquished her child to adoption, the early days after reunion are like an intense love affair. Though it's not coloured by sexual desire, you think of the other person all the time. You look forward to the next time you will be with them, you constantly want to hug them, you notice how soft their skin is and how tender the back of their neck looks, and you long to reach out and touch that spot. You hang on to every word they say, no matter how mundane. You study their features when you think they are not looking. You look for hidden meanings in the most simple statements and words.

During the exhilarating early days of our reunion, I wrote about my intense feelings for Billy. It is somewhat overwrought, but if you have gone through a reunion you'll recognize and understand the passion and infatuation:

I'm remembering the second time we met at my house. . . . Just before you left to go back to your friends, I suddenly started to cry and I put my head on the kitchen table to gain control of myself. I felt embarrassed. I didn't want you to have to deal with this sudden eruption of emotion. You were sitting close to me and you put your hand on my arm and asked if I was all right. It melted my heart, but steadied me too. I looked up, wiped my eyes, smiled and said, "Yes, I'm fine, just fine. It's been an emotional day, that's all." I couldn't look at you because I was feeling so overwhelmed and raw. Then you got up to go to the door and I went to you and hugged you tight. I nestled my face in your neck and kissed it. I took a deep breath and took in your odour and you smelled wonderful. I kissed your face and then almost forgot and nearly kissed your mouth. We both laughed at the near miss and then you kissed me back. I said fiercely, "I still love you." And you said, "That's good to know," and hugged me tighter. Then at the door I kissed you again and grabbed your hand and squeezed for dear life. "Don't leave me," I wanted to plead, "oh, please don't go.". . . Every time I see you, I want something from you impossible to grasp; impossible to ask for and expect. Simply put, I want you to be my baby again. I thought when I found you the cruel tightly coiled spring in the pit of my stomach had come undone, but now I had discovered it would never be completely gone. The last little bit will never spring free because I lost my baby—the never being able to hold you, kiss you good night, nurture you, kiss your scrapes and bruises, watch you grow, help shape you. It was all irretrievably gone. Nothing in the world can change that and the regret and longing will never completely go away.

Then I wrote: "I know he likes it that I love him and want to be with him all the time. He's glad I found him but he does not love me and share the some longing I have for him. How could he?"

Over time, those emotions became less raw. The all-consuming grief over a missed past diminished and the crazy love died down. Billy and I became part of the fabric of each other's lives.

The summer of 1998, before his last year of university at Waterloo, Billy got a job in Toronto and came to live with me. The previous year,

Doug and I had separated after seventeen years together, and I was living alone in a little house in the South Riverdale area. Sharing this small space, Billy and I really got to know each other. On many a night, I'd come home from a meeting or a political event, and we would sit in the living room, sipping brandy and talking until the wee hours.

Billy was diagnosed with childhood diabetes when he was nine years old. When he turned eighteen he applied to the Children's Aid Society for non-identifying information, hoping to obtain the medical background of his birth parents. He showed me the package provided to him, labelled "Family Background History." This document contained information that the social worker assigned to my case had written about me:

> Physically, your birth mother was described as 5' tall, weighing 100 lbs. She had brown hair, blue grey eyes, a fair complexion and a slight build. Your birth mother was described as a petite, shy looking girl, and fairly pretty. She was a neat stylish dresser—a small serious looking girl.
>
> Personality wise your birth mother was described as a quiet spoken girl, very warm and honest when approached. She was quite independent.... She was very sincere and sensitive which partly accounted for her shyness. She was realistic in looking at herself and her problems, mature but unsure of her future.

It was interesting to see that I had told my social worker nice things about his father. She had written that I said he was well liked and a very considerate person, intelligent and soft-spoken, and extremely kind. Unfortunately for Billy, there was practically no family health information. I knew almost nothing about Chris's family and, at the time, there was no significant health information to recount about my family either.

Billy, Astra, and her son, James.

It was also fascinating to read someone's impression of me when I was so young. Though I did harrumph when I read the bit describing me as only "fairly" pretty.

Billy brought me pictures of his past, starting from the day his adoptive parents brought him home. When we looked at them together, I gave each one a cursory glance, moving quickly through the albums. But when I was alone, I examined each photo carefully, taking in every last detail until I thought my heart would explode. Every time I looked at them, I wound up wallowing in my old sorrow and I would have to put the album away. Perhaps one day I will be able to look at the pictures without the old wounds opening up.

I realized I would never be my child's mother in the way I would be if I had raised him, and nothing in the world could change that. So there was only one thing to do: I came to terms with it, with life as it was.

Billy spent a lot of time in the evenings hanging out and playing music with my new partner, Richard, who at the time was the executive director of the White Ribbon campaign and later became Jack Layton's executive assistant. Billy plays the piano and guitar and has a beautiful singing voice, and Richard plays guitar and saxophone, so music was a great way for them to get to know each other. And Billy and his newly discovered sister, Astra, and her son, James, spent a great deal of time together and became close. Although I didn't see it and she didn't realize it herself at the time, thrilled as she was to have her brother in her life, Astra was having a hard time sharing her mom.

Eventually, I got to meet Billy's brother and sister and their kids, too. They are his family—the people who raised him and with whom he grew up, the people who love him and whom he loves. They therefore became very special people to me.

FIFTEEN

SO IT BEGINS

I **WAS IN A** unique position to fight for legislative change. It doesn't get much more inside than a seat as an elected official in the legislature. But when I began my efforts in the late 1990s, plenty of skilled and knowledgeable people were already involved who brought decades of experience to the battle. Their knowledge, organizing abilities, and commitment were the driving force behind my actions in the legislature.

Toronto's Parent Finders Inc. and other Parent Finders groups from across the province lobbied the government for changes to adoption disclosure legislation throughout the 1980s and into the 1990s. Parent Finders had been founded in Vancouver in 1974. Founder Joan Vanstone, an adoptee, had said that nothing would change "until adoptees got up on their hind legs and worked for change." A group of adoptees took Vanstone's advice and, as a result, in 1996, British Columbia was the first province in Canada to open up its adoption records.

In Toronto in the early 1990s, Parent Finders staged many protests on the lawns of Queen's Park and set up meetings with every member of the NDP government, as well as with the opposition Liberals and Progressive Conservatives. They put together fact sheets and presented papers that showed how well adoption disclosure reform was working in other jurisdictions. Eventually, cabinet came through with its support of Tony Martin's private member's bill in May 1994. But adoption activists were disappointed in the NDP government for waiting until so late in its mandate to deal with the issue, and they were devastated when the opposition filibuster prevented a final vote on Martin's bill.

But they remained undaunted. Despite the huge setback, they could see that the work on Martin's bill had created momentum, and that support for reform had grown among legislators and the public. They continued to work hard to keep that momentum going.

Holly Kramer, who had been instrumental in my reunion with Billy, helped me tremendously when I introduced my first bill. She had been a board member of Parent Finders Inc. for a number of years and served as president from 1994 to 2000.

Bill 88 was the first of five disclosure bills I brought before the legislature between 1998 and 2005. It was titled, rather prosaically, Adoption Disclosure Statute Law Amendment Act, 1998. As with Martin's 1994 bill, Bill 88 would have allowed an adopted person who was at least eighteen years old to obtain a copy of the original registration of their birth and a copy of the registered adoption order, without requiring the birth mother to have signed on. The bill did not go so far as to allow birth parents the same ability to acquire information without consent of the adoptee.

In formulating our early bills, both Martin and I knew that allowing birth parents the same opportunity would have been seen as a much more drastic step, and we feared that including it could stand in the way of the bill's progress. General public consensus focused at that point on the rights of adoptees to unlock their information. But both of our bills did eliminate the mandatory government counselling that had been written into the old law. Counselling overseen by the government would, rather, be available upon request.

Alex Cullen, a member of the Liberal party (who later joined the NDP) and himself an adoptive father, introduced a similar bill for first reading on June 10, 1998. His bill would have given birth parents access to their children's original birth information. However, because the adoption community felt that my bill stood a better chance of receiving all-party support, Cullen graciously withdrew the bill he had worked so hard on and threw his support behind mine. I still have the folder containing a copy of his bill that he distributed at the time of first reading. I hold it dear, because Cullen's deep commitment to justice for adoptees and birth parents, like Martin's, was an important step along the way to victory.

Bill 88 was introduced in the legislature on December 2, 1998, just before the house would recess for the Christmas break. It was scheduled for second reading—and the first opportunity for debate—on December 10. A couple of days before that, I held a press conference with Holly Kramer and Michael Grand (his birth name; at the time he was known as Michael Sobol), professor of psychology and co-director of the National Adoption Study of Canada. These were two of the country's most knowledgeable people on the subject, and both had personal experience with adoption and reunion. I relied on their guidance when I wrote the bill and they were there with me every step of the way.

Some of the media seemed to get it. To our delight, Ian Urquhart, who had become the *Toronto Star*'s provincial affairs columnist, wrote an informative and supportive column. Thus began the process of educating the public, MPPs, and the media and of debunking some of the most common fears and myths.

At the press conference, Holly Kramer pointed out that Bill 88 reflected a consensus within the adoption community and was in line with academic findings and the recommendations of two major government commissions and four cross-province consultations of the last two decades. Grand discussed his extensive research on adoption and explained that "the desire to know of one's origins is neither a rejection of adoptive parents nor a sign of the failure of the adoption. It reflects the need of all of us to build a full sense of personal identity; like non-adoptees, adopted persons must have access to 'chapter one' of their lives."

At the time Bill 88 was introduced, we were able to point to a plethora of global jurisdictions that had already opened their adoption records. We weren't inventing the wheel. Not one of these jurisdictions reported veto violations or any significant problems after their adoption records were open.

When Bill 88 came up for second reading debate, I had ten minutes to present my case. We had completed our consultations and lobbying, sent packages to all 103 members of legislature, and spent hours on the phone and visiting individual members to explain the bill and answer their questions. I knew where the votes were, and I was confident I had majority support.

By coincidence, December 10 was Human Rights Day, so I began with this: "I think it's appropriate and a very good omen today that this bill is up for debate on International Human Rights Day. We have a chance today to recognize the human rights of all persons within Ontario and bring Ontario in line with the UN conventions on human rights and rights of the child and the Canadian charter." I did my best in those precious ten minutes to convince members that my bill was modest and that I had made compromises in order to gain support from all parties.

After I spoke, members from all three parties took turns responding to my remarks. The first speaker was Progressive Conservative Frank Klees, who, the Hansard transcripts show, spoke in favour of the bill: "Is it appropriate for a system to be in place that hides important information about a person's background from them for life?

I don't believe so. I believe that we as a society, as a legislature, need to do what we can to take the barriers down to ensure that everyone in the province has that access, that right and that opportunity." Unfortunately, come 2005, during a debate on the Liberal government bill on the same topic, Klees would play a different tune.

The next speaker was Liberal Dominic Agostino, who would die in 2004 of liver cancer at the age of forty-three. He was my kind of politician—a passionate street fighter (as most Hamilton politicians seem to be) and a hard worker. He could be partisan on many issues, but his support of adoption disclosure rights never wavered. Agostino was very generous that morning in his praise for my work on this issue.

My colleague Tony Silipo, who had worked with me on Tony Martin's private member's bill, spoke eloquently. Silipo would die in 2012 of brain cancer, only fifty-three years old. He had served as chair of the management board, minister of education, and minister of community and social services in the NDP government. He was one of the most thoughtful guys I've met, a superb parliamentarian, and a man of integrity whose commitment to adoption disclosure reform will be remembered.

We also received enthusiastic support during the debate from Liberals Alex Cullen, Gerry Phillips, and David Ramsay, and of course, from Tony Martin. Many of these people had personal experience with the issue: Cullen was an adoptive father; Ramsay, an adoptee. New Democratic MPP Gilles Bisson spoke movingly about uniting with his birth sister.

One of my archenemies spoke as well, the only member of the legislature to speak against the bill that day. Progressive Conservative David Tilson (now a federal member of Parliament) stalked me through every bill until he was defeated in the 2003 election. He demonstrated the flipside of how personal experience can influence a member on a piece of legislation. Tilson said that his wife was adopted and had a negative reunion experience; ergo, no one else should be encouraged or helped.

When the time for debate was over, I had a few minutes to sum up. I looked over at my son, who was sitting in the gallery, and then, to demonstrate that it wasn't only birth mothers and adoptees that saw the need to open adoption records, I read from a letter sent by an adoptive father. He wrote:

> We believe if our children are loved and cared for, we do not have to be afraid of their searching, for those reunions will only help them become more settled and become more satisfied human beings. Our love for our son and his love for us has not diminished since this reunion but only grown as his mind and heart are at peace.

I then expressed my appreciation for the comments and concerns from all my colleagues. I told Tilson that I had sympathy for anyone who had a bad reunion experience, but that that should not stop our quest for the right of every human being to have information about themselves. I tried to make it personal to the legislators, asking, "Can you imagine how you'd feel if you knew somebody had secret information in a document about you and you couldn't get your hands on it?"

I ended the debate by expressing my disappointment that I would not, as I had hoped, have unanimous consent to move third reading and allow the bill to be passed into law. I asked members from both sides of the house to help move the bill forward quickly by making it a priority within their caucuses so that together we could ensure we didn't let down the adoption community again.

I could hear the desperation in my voice and words. The vote was fifty-three for and three against. The bill was referred to the Standing Committee on Social Development, but it never made it to their agenda—an agenda that the governing majority Progressive Conservatives controlled. Again, the legislature let the community down, and the bill would die on the order paper. But it didn't die without a fight.

It became clear that the house was going to prorogue; prorogation meant a new session of parliament and Bill 88 would be dead unless it was carried over. I made frantic attempts to persuade the house leaders to include Bill 88 in an agreed-upon package of bills to be carried over. I wrote to Janet Ecker, the minister of community and social services, asking her to try to persuade the Progressive Conservative house leader to keep the bill alive.

We had good reason to be concerned, because the government house leader happened to be Norm Sterling—one of the instigators who had stopped Tony Martin's bill from passing in 1994. To be fair to Sterling, I did get his verbal commitment to include it in an agreed-upon package of bills to be carried into the next session. Whether he would have kept that commitment we'll never know, because the session ended on a sour note with bickering over a sex scandal involving the former Speaker Al McLean. The legislative sitting ended at the prescribed time of midnight, December 17, without passing Sterling's motion to carry over certain bills. I still held out some hope because the government did not prorogue that evening as expected. But they did it quietly the next day by order in council. It was over.

After the demise of the bill, I wrote to supporters to thank them for their hard work and to express my sorrow that we had again been unsuccessful. But I asked them to continue their advocacy work by contacting the minister and Premier Mike Harris and demanding that the house be reconvened and the bill be brought back. However, I ended on a realistic note: "I hope very much that Bill 88 can still be passed but if we fail once again, we can take solace in having moved legislative and public support significantly in our favour."

Even though Bill 88 was gone, we had high hopes that the government might move forward on adoption disclosure reform. That's because I had had positive conversations with the minister of community and social services and she had promised that she would consider allowing adoptees access to their birth records. Minister Ecker honestly seemed to get it. But to my dismay, shortly after our conversation, people from the adoption community began receiving letters from her that omitted any reference to reforms and instead dwelled upon improving waiting times.

I felt like I'd gone through a time warp. Here we were back to square one again. But we did not lose all hope. I understood that Ecker must have had to put up with a lot in that old boys' caucus of hers, but she was pretty tough. If anyone could find a way to defy them, she would be the one. So I got a shock when I was sent Ecker's response to a letter she received in December 1998 in support of Bill 88. Her letter, dated February 2, 1999, indicated that Bill 88 had died on the order paper in December 1998 and that she had no intention of moving forward with any reforms; rather, she would focus on improving services and wait times.

I was taken by surprise and immediately sent her an irate letter and issued a press release. The letter began:

Dear Ms. Ecker, I read with dismay and shock a copy of your letter to Mr. Kenneth Bruder who wrote to you on December 16, 1998 regarding my Private Members Bill 88, Adoption Disclosure Statute Law Amendment Act. You have indicated to me on several occasions that you support the need for adoption disclosure reform in this province. Indeed, at one point you suggested that you were looking at making changes under the Child and Family Services Act. It was only when you introduced amendments to this act, Bill 73, Child and

Family Services Amendment Act, 1998, without adoption reform included that I put forward a private members bill.

I went on to point out that fixing the existing system is not the issue; that it was not working and we needed to make real changes.

The issue was picking up steam in the media, which helped energize the community's efforts. The *Toronto Star* published an excellent opinion piece by Debbie Rolph entitled "Time the law treated grown adopted people as adults." Michele Landsberg wrote two pieces in the *Star* urging the government to open adoption records. John Ibbitson from the *National Post* even got in on the action with an article entitled "Tories backtrack on allowing adoptees access to records."

Meanwhile, as the political process was going on, I had personal struggles of my own to confront as well.

SIXTEEN

BETWEEN A ROCK
AND A HARD PLACE

THOUGHT I'D ALWAYS keep Billy a secret from my parents. I knew that if I ever told them, there would be an uproar. My father would be angry and I was afraid that he would take it out on my mother. I had a selfish reason, too. Having been the black sheep of the family, my election to public office had redeemed me in my father's eyes. (Not quite so much in my mother's; by her standards, I was still a pretty lousy housekeeper.) My father was so proud of my accomplishments; I didn't want to ruin my new status by shaming him and tainting his pride in me.

Like Joni Mitchell, who had kept her pregnancy a secret, too, I knew how scandalous the whole thing would have been to my parents. Mitchell said in an interview with the *Los Angeles Times* on August 8, 1997: "The main thing at the time was to conceal it. The scandal was so intense. A daughter could do nothing more disgraceful. It ruined you in a social sense. You have no idea what the stigma was. It was like you murdered somebody."

Where I grew up, when an unwed girl got pregnant the whole family was shamed. The parents were blamed, and the poor girl was the subject of gossip, scorn, and pity. My parents were good Christian people who took pride in the way they raised their family and had a rather narrow moral universe. Once, my paternal grandmother included in a letter a piece of paper folded and taped into a small square. My mother whisked it away, out of sight. But I saw her slip it into the cutlery drawer, no doubt to read later when we were out of sight. I was so curious that the minute she went to the store, I slipped it out of the drawer and picked off enough of the tape to read it.

"Remember the Joneses who lived down the lane by Reg's store?" it said. "Well, their daughter Bertha is going to have a baby and she is *not married*. Everyone knows she was fooling around with that Joe from the Lower End and he's disappeared."

I was thrilled to know the secret, and I immediately realized that this was the worst thing that could happen to a girl and her family. Even now, I didn't want my family to be one of "those families." But I also wanted to put Billy's needs first, even if that meant causing me and others distress. I asked Billy whether it was important to him to meet his grandparents. He didn't hesitate. I heard the deep yearning in his voice when he replied, "Yes, at the very least I want them to know I exist. But if possible, I would like to meet them."

I did not let on just how difficult a task he had set out for me. Now I would have to tell my parents that I had done that terrible thing. Taking a deep breath, I told him that I would arrange a meeting the next time they came to Toronto. A few months later, in February 1999, they arrived at my house for their annual visit. I had ten days. Several went by and still I could not find the right moment or the right words.

With two days left before they were to leave, time was running out. I would have to tell them. All that morning, I caught myself unconsciously singing "Jesus Loves Me, This I Know," a hymn we had sung as children. I had become a frightened child again. I had by now revealed my secret to my brothers and sisters, and I had shared that I was going to tell our parents on this visit. That day, while trying to get up my nerve, I went upstairs several times to phone each of them in turn, secretly hoping that one of them would talk me out of it. But they all supported me and encouraged me to go ahead.

By mid-morning, I still had not summoned the courage. I thought of Billy, and of my promise to him. I knew that I really had to do it.

My parents, who loved the game of curling, were contentedly watching a semifinal match—my father on the couch, my mother in a chair close by the TV. They were both hard of hearing, so the volume was turned way up. I sat down in a chair beside my mother, facing them both.

I took a deep breath. All my rehearsed words went out the window. They looked at me wondering what I wanted.

"Turn down the TV," I yelled. "I have something important to tell you."

They looked alarmed. I was on edge, and I could see in their eyes that they thought I was going to give them some terrible news. I grabbed the remote out of my father's hand and muted the TV. To calm them, I shouted, "Don't worry; it's not serious."

They look relieved.

"But, still, it's going to shock you, so be prepared."

The looks of alarm reappeared.

Oh God, I thought, *my father has had six heart bypasses and I'm killing him.*

"You have a grandson that you don't know about," I bellowed.

"What?" they said in unison.

They looked bewildered. They didn't get it. Maybe they didn't hear me.

I can't do this, I thought.

I repeated it a little louder: "You have a grandson you don't know about."

Their shocked looks were even worse than I'd imagined they'd be. But there was no turning back.

I told about getting pregnant the first year I left home, giving up my baby for adoption, and the joy I was experiencing in having recently found him. I explained that Billy was now a big part of my life and that their grandson wanted to meet them.

This was so hard, I could hardly bear it. Then, to my amazement, my father turned back toward the TV, turned the volume way up, and said, calmly: "Look at that rock, Myrtis."

I couldn't believe it. I turned off the TV, and in my confused despair, I waited for one of them to say something, anything. My father's jaw was clenched and he looked angry. My mother had turned pale and looked utterly stricken.

But it was over. I had done it.

I went upstairs to call my older sister, Edna. I told her that it was as bad as could be and that she should call our parents soon to try to calm them down. I came back down in time to hear my father say to my mother: "Pack your bags, Myrtis. We're going home."

I was no longer panic-stricken. Now, I was just plain angry. I said to Doug, "I'm going to go help them pack and you can take them to the airport. I want nothing more to do with them."

Then my mother, who was always the dutiful spouse to my father, surprised me.

"No, Eddie," she stated firmly. "He is our grandson and we're going to stay here and meet him."

Suddenly, the shock of all that has just happened kicked in. I went back upstairs and sat on my bed, shaking and worrying about what my next move should be.

My mother came upstairs, sat down beside me, and said with a great deal of emotion, "Oh my, Marilyn, you must have gone through an awful time. I wish you could have told me."

This meant a lot to me. My mother was not one to show me a lot of empathy or to stand up to my father. Among all of her children, I had the most difficult relationship with her, but she came through when I needed her most. I saw a determination and strength that I had never seen before. I thanked her and gave her a big hug.

I showed her pictures of Billy, which she studied for a long time. Then she told me that, no matter what, she would make sure Billy got to meet them. She wanted to meet her grandson just as badly as he wanted to meet her. She was enormously curious about him, and as she scrutinized his features looking for family resemblances, she commented on how good-looking he was and stated firmly that he looked like her side of the family.

Eventually we went back downstairs and I asked my father to go for a walk. It was a warm, sunny day; we walked for blocks without saying a word. Someone had to make a move, so finally I gently took his arm and said that I was sorry I had caused him such distress. That was the best apology I was able to give.

He did not remove my hand, but he remained silent. As we approached the house, he looked at me and said, "Well, he is our grandson, so I guess we will have to meet him." These were basically my mother's words, but what a relief to hear them from my father's mouth.

Billy was back in university in Waterloo. I phoned to tell him that I had told my parents about him, and invited him to come to meet them. The next day, he walked in my door and there they were face to face, my parents and their first grandchild! My mother smiled at him and gave him a hug. My father was more reserved but did look

Billy meets his maternal grandparents for the first time.

hard at him when he shook his hand, as though he was searching for a family resemblance.

Astra and James dropped in. I made tea, and we sat in the living room and made polite conversation for a while. The conversation was a bit strained. But, at long last, we were all together in the same room. Astra took pictures of the four of us sitting together on the couch.

After Billy left, my parents and I carried on as though nothing extraordinary had just happened. I did catch my father complaining to my mother that Billy was sporting a little earring. And I giggled as I heard my mother say, "But Eddy, Fred"—my youngest brother—"wears earrings in both his ears." That settled that.

SEVENTEEN

A TUMULTUOUS YEAR

THE YEAR 2000 was a tough one for me. My father was showing signs of dementia and eventually was diagnosed with Alzheimer's disease. He was in the early stages, but it was getting too difficult for my mother to manage him on her own in their little house in Carbonear. My sister Edna's husband, Jim, had been lured away to Maine to practise medicine, so none of us were there to lend a hand. That summer, the five siblings convened in Carbonear, and we used all our persuasive powers to get them to agree to spend at least winters with their children. My father wanted none of it, but eventually he relented. Edna flew with them to visit my brother Max in Winnipeg, after which she took them to Prince Rupert for an extended stay with my sister Joan and her husband, Keith.

My father became very ill in Prince Rupert and was airlifted to a Victoria hospital. Once again we came from all over to be with him. He was pretty out of it by then, but he recognized us most of the time. Between us, we spent almost every hour with him in the hospital. When doctors made it clear to us that his heart was failing and there was nothing further they could do, I said my last goodbyes to him and went home. My sister Joan and my mother brought him back to Prince Rupert, where he died a few weeks later.

Meanwhile, I was as busy as ever in the legislature. I introduced a new adoption disclosure bill—Bill 108—in June. This bill had a significant addition: it provided for access to birth registrations and records for birth parents as well as for adoptees. We had reluctantly left out this right for birth parents in my first bill, because we were hoping to have a better chance of success by going with just the rights of adoptees. But since that attempt had failed, we were determined to broaden the scope of disclosure to benefit both adoptees and birth parents.

Three people in particular influenced this change—Karen Lynn, Wendy Rowney, and Dr. Michael Grand. Karen Lynn cut her teeth in the women's movement. She is a completely engaged teacher of English as a second language, with an acerbic wit and a sharp mind. Passionate and full of energy, she threw herself into the adoption disclosure battle in 1995 when she started her search for her son Doug. After reuniting with him in 1999, she became an even more determined activist for adoption disclosure reform.

Rowney, a supervisor of public programming at a large history museum, is a kind and gentle woman who speaks with a calm determination. She is a natural leader who is good at cheerfully organizing people into action. An adoptee herself who found her birth mother in 1997, her feelings ran deep and passionate, but she kept a cool head and voice throughout the long process of reforming Ontario's adoption laws.

I had met Grand when I introduced Bill 88 two years earlier, and I had been mightily impressed. He had a big personality and a big laugh, and lent a booming, authoritative voice to the cause. He was skilled at researching and writing, as well as at speaking publicly at press conferences. Grand's story is a little different. His father died when he was six years old, but after he was adopted by his stepfather, his family never talked about his biological dad and the adoption.

This experience made him a passionate advocate for openness in adoption.

Lynn, Rowney, and Grand got together and soon realized that they shared a common vision—a willingness to seek compromise and a firm commitment to achieve open records for both adopted adults and birth parents. And they felt that their combined history as a birth mother, an adoptee, and an adoption professional who was also an adoptee could be very effective.

The trio was influenced by a national online discussion forum called CanAdopt, which was started in 1996 by a group of adoptees who discovered the power of the internet to communicate with each other. For the first time, Canadian adopted people and birth parents were able to talk to each other about their shared history in a forum controlled by them without direction from any government or its representatives. And among the many issues, there was one they all agreed on—the need for open records.

On the CanAdopt site, Lynn at last found a voice for mothers who had surrendered their children for adoption. In late 1999, she started an internet organization for birth mothers to talk about their losses and reunions, and their pain and rage, and to direct their newfound voices toward disclosure reform.

That voice became more powerful than she had dreamt! Lynn founded the Canadian Council of Birth Mothers (later changed to the Canadian Council of Natural Mothers, or ccnm) on Mother's Day 2000. The mothers raised their voices nationally and began to put to rest the harmful myths and stereotypes about the million women in Canada who had lost their children to adoption. These women discovered there were many just like them who had been powerless young women in a callous and indifferent society that had shunned and shamed them. They found strength in each other and came up with strategies on how to change the way society viewed them. Mature

Canadian women began to come out of the closet in letters to the editor, on radio and TV, and to their families and friends. They joined with adult adoptees in the quest to open sealed adoption records.

Founders of COAR—Wendy Rowney, Karen Lynn, and Michael Grand (aka Santa!)—with Ann Fessler (2nd from left).

One night as Lynn, Rowney, and Grand sat around Lynn's kitchen table discussing strategy, a new organization was born. They gave themselves a straightforward name: the Coalition for Open Adoption Records. COAR became instrumental in the successful effort to change Ontario's laws.

At the time, an active volunteer network of Parent Finders groups across the province helped adoptees and birth parents with search and reunion issues. Although this was their main focus, they also supported open adoption records and had been at the forefront of all efforts to reform Ontario's laws. This network was completely on board.

Lynn, Rowney, and Grand knew that they must have a unified voice if they were to speak out publicly, and that meant they first needed the support of the entire Ontario adoption community. This was before email was widely accessible; they spent every spare minute phoning and writing to every adoption group in the province introducing COAR and asking for each group's endorsement. They got it!

Now they were able to say they represented every adoption group in the province, which allowed them to speak with authority on the issue. At that point, COAR contacted me. I was delighted to learn there was an umbrella group that I could work with. Soon after COAR was established, we met in my office in the legislature to establish common ground on who should be granted access to information, and this included birth parents.

Over the next few years, the three of them were active everywhere on adoption reform. They worked to improve understanding of the issues within the adoption community and among MPPs. They joined boards of adoption organizations, worked with leaders of the Ontario Association of Children's Aid Societies, spoke at conferences, sat on committees, and drummed up support from the medical community, which recognized the medical consequences of secret adoption records. They researched adoption history in Ontario and became experts in adoption laws in other jurisdictions. They attended every reading of every adoption bill in Ontario. They spoke at standing committee hearings and met with ministers. They held a reception for MPPs at Queen's Park, distributed information packages to every member, and organized a rally on the legislature steps. Amazingly, they did all of this while working at regular full-time jobs.

Lynn mobilized the mothers of CCNM to write letters to politicians and the media, and to visit their representatives. The defence of sealed records so often offered by legislators—that birth mothers were promised confidentiality—began to crumble under the barrage of testimony from incensed mothers who would no longer allow uninformed elected representatives to rewrite their own histories. Not one member of CCNM *ever* came forward to say that she had been offered confidentiality. In fact, these mothers came to understand that confidentiality was a condition for surrender, not a promise. Lynn said to me at the time, "The rage of mothers who had been oppressed, lied to, and profoundly offended by the combined systems of the social work profession, the churches, doctors and nurses, and the law was finally being unleashed."

Changes had been made in the provincial legislature, too. My riding of Riverdale was renamed Toronto–Danforth to reflect its newly expanded boundaries, and John Baird (now Canada's foreign affairs minister) was sworn in as the new minister of community and social services in 1999. I was thrilled. He had been a strong supporter of Bill 88, and having him in this position gave me renewed hope.

Second reading for Bill 108 was scheduled for November 23, 2000, and all of us were gearing up for it. I continued to work closely with Holly Kramer from Parent Finders and with Lynn, Rowney, and Grand from COAR, as well as with Joan Vanstone and Jim Kelly from British Columbia, who had generously helped me prepare Bill 88 and continued to provide advice and encouragement. With this amazing team in place, I honestly felt we would not fail this time.

However, second reading never took place. This bill was held up not by the usual shenanigans in the legislature, but by the Walkerton E. coli tainted water tragedy. In May 2000, a month before I introduced Bill 108, a terrible chain of events led to the deaths of seven people, including a two-year-old girl, and to hundreds becoming seriously ill in an Ontario small town. This crisis took precedence over everything else. As the New Democratic environment critic, I had been warning the government for months that there could be serious consequences to their deep budget cuts to the Ministry of the Environment, deregulation, and downloading of many responsibilities from the province to municipalities.

After the terrible event, I was consumed with the issue for months and spent as much time as possible in Walkerton, meeting with the people who were directly affected. Working with them and with environmental organizations, I put my energy into establishing comprehensive safe drinking water legislation. I introduced my Safe Drinking Water Act—Bill 96—in the hope that strong legislation would prevent such a tragedy from recurring. Eventually, Bill 96 died on the order paper, but because of the strong, sustained support it drew and pressure to take meaningful action in response to the

Walkerton tragedy, the government eventually brought in its own Safe Drinking Water Act that addressed some of the key issues identified in my bill.

Unfortunately, however, the government did not deal with my other private member's bill, and in December, Bill 108 died on the order paper when the house prorogued. This meant we would have to start all over again in the next session. The good news, though, was that the movement for reform now had a powerful new addition—the voices of the mothers.

EIGHTEEN

SURVIVAL IS TO BEGIN AGAIN

S O ONCE MORE, we started over. I introduced my third bill—Bill 77—on June 6, 2001. Of the five attempts, this is the bill that came closest to being passed. And even though (surprise, surprise) the house was eventually prorogued without the bill being voted on, the progress toward adoption disclosure proved to be significant. It gave the issue momentum in that vast open space that is public opinion.

Unlike my first two bills, Bill 77 reached the committee hearing stage, something that gave both supporters and opponents a chance to fully air their views. It is very rare for opposition private members' bills to be allowed public hearings; I had to bargain long and hard with the government to get them. I was on government members' cases every day—in the legislature, in the corridors of Queen's Park, and on the airwaves—and my persistence paid off. The hearings were granted. Supporters devised publicity campaigns and public demonstrations. The media became engaged and gave the hearings significant coverage.

Opposition mainly focused on the issue of privacy. Would a law that allowed the disclosure of information that had been kept secret contravene the privacy rights of women who had years ago given up children for adoption? How many of those mothers in fact yearned for an end to that state-imposed privacy so that they could be found by their lost children? Should the rights of adoptees who needed to know, among other things, the medical histories of their birth parents trump any privacy rights of those parents? Finally, would opening up the information but allowing all parties to declare limits on contact with other involved parties satisfy privacy concerns?

As we were preparing Bill 77, we knew that the provincial privacy commissioner in British Columbia had vigorously opposed allowing reformed adoption information laws to be retroactive. In other words, the privacy commissioner felt that information should be open as of the date the legislation took effect, but the law should not apply to information that had heretofore been kept private. Notwithstanding the views of the privacy commissioner, British Columbia allowed release of information retroactively when it passed its adoption disclosure bill in 1995. (Later, when Newfoundland and Labrador and Alberta would consider such reforms, their privacy commissioners also opposed retroactively. But both provinces went ahead with retroactive disclosure bills).

We were concerned that, even though Ontario's privacy commissioner, Ann Cavoukian, had no legal jurisdiction over the matter, we could be blindsided if the government decided to solicit her views on the bill and make them public. I decided to be proactive and meet with her. I hoped that, if necessary, I could sway her by pointing to the success of disclosure reform in jurisdictions where open adoption records had by then been the norm for years. In the end, Cavoukian did submit an opinion in a letter to me on October 1, 2001. She stated her concerns regarding retroactivity, but conceded that "the appropriate balance between access and privacy" in this case would likely "ultimately be determined by social policy considerations."

Nevertheless, we were worried. With the privacy commissioner expressing concern about retroactivity and the rights of biological mothers to privacy, the opponents of Bill 77, including government MPPs, had some strong new ammunition. And we were right to be worried. Her concerns were raised repeatedly by members who were opposed to retroactivity. During committee hearings held on November 5 and 7 and December 5, 2001, chaired by Progressive Conservative Steve Gilchrist, we had to debunk a number of myths.

Norm Miller, who had supported my previous bills, now spoke cautiously as the official representative of the government position. He dwelled on the government's commitment to help reunite families more effectively and quickly through the present system. That was what I expected from the government side.

But next up was Ernie Parsons. To my surprise, even though he was not officially on the committee, he gave the opening statement for the Liberal caucus. Parsons was a sincere, pleasant man who was highly regarded. I knew his position on my bill would have influence, and he strenuously opposed the reforms. Parsons explained passionately why he was unable to support the retroactivity of the bill. He spoke of his two adopted sisters, of being a former chair and board member of the Children's Aid Society, and of being a foster parent for many years. Even though his personal and professional experiences were impressive, he had no statistics or data to back up his claims. No matter. He touched upon all of the myths about adoption disclosure, and he was very persuasive. His words made an impression on committee members and on the media, and it was not a good one for our side.

Parsons said he had received letters, calls, and visits from birth mothers who "were in great distress at the possibility of an individual showing up at their door and identifying themselves as their birth child." He said some of them had commitments in writing from Children's Aid that their names would never be released.

We knew this was not possible. No doubt some women were given verbal assurances, but despite a widely repeated myth to the contrary, no such commitments were ever made in writing. And those assurances worked the other way, too. Many women said they had been assured by their social workers and other officials that they would be able to reunite once their children became adults, and that assurance had given them some comfort when they lost their babies.

Parsons also said that, while some adoption reunions worked out well, many didn't, and the people involved say, in hindsight, that they wished they had never happened. Again he had no statistics, but he was very persuasive.

Then Parsons ventured into territory that few dared to speak of, but that I knew was a great concern to some middle-aged men who were opposed to the bill. He said that birth mothers, when they gave their babies up for adoption, were asked for the name of the birth father, and that any name they gave was registered as the father. "There was never any check done, and I suspect at times there were young men listed who had no knowledge of it whatsoever and may or may not have been the birth father."

Aha. There it was—out in the open at last. Some of these men were against disclosure reform because they were afraid that children they had fathered or may have fathered who had been adopted might come knocking on their doors.

Parsons set the tone for the hearings, and it was up to a who's who of adoption activists to counter the arguments . We heard from Monica Byrne for Ottawa Parent Finders; Patricia McCarron for the Adoption Reform Coalition; Holly Kramer and Brian Macdonald for Parent Finders Inc.; Michael Grand for the Adoption Council of Ontario; Natalie Proctor Servant for Bastard Nation; Mary Shields for Birthmothers for Each Other; Patricia Fenton for Families in Adoption; Marvin Bernstein and Mary Allan for Ontario's Association of

Children's Aid Societies; and Wendy Rowney for the Coalition for Open Adoption Records. Karen Lynn—reunited with her son Doug, who was by her side on his thirty-eighth birthday—testified for the Canadian Council of Birth Mothers. We heard from individuals such as Donna Marie Marchand, a First Nation adoptee activist; Dianne Mathes, a reunited adoptee and adoption therapist; Kariann Ford, an adoptee with a serious inherited medical condition; and Terry Gardiner, a reunited adoptee from Quebec. Each of them delivered strong, knowledgeable, and, at times, emotional remarks to the committee.

The Ontario Children's Aid Society spokespeople came out firmly in support of the bill. Wendy Rowney, an adoptee, countered Parsons' concern over disappointing reunions.

> When we make the decision to encounter our pasts, we know we may not like what we find. Despite childhood fantasies, we know that the very fact we were surrendered for adoption means there were problems surrounding our birth, conception and perhaps childhood. We know that not all endings are happy. Independently, we decide the need to know is greater than the fear of what we may find. This is an adult decision, made after a great deal of deliberation and soul-searching. It is not something we enter into lightly. As adults, adoptees can and do make decisions every day, even momentous ones which may alter how we see the world and our place in it. Like all adults making life-changing decisions, adopted persons have the ability to make these decisions on their own. We are no longer children, and we do not wish to be treated as such.

Monica Byrne, who had been an adoption disclosure activist since the 1970s, told of how she gave up her first child, a daughter, for adoption in 1966 simply because she wasn't married. "I gave her away strictly because it was 1966. I was in university. I was unmarried. My husband-to-be was in university. Being an unwed mother in 1966 was not on. . . . You didn't keep a child out of wedlock. Period."

She later married that child's father, and they had three other children. Her first child "was just as much my child as my other three children, only she was not with me," Byrne said. "She was with another family. . . . It didn't mean I didn't care. It didn't mean I didn't love her.'

"I was never promised confidentiality," Byrne told the legislators. "I never requested confidentiality. I filled in no forms. I was asked to fill in no forms. . . . I was told, in fact, at the time when my daughter turned 18, I would be able to find her. . . . I held that memory in my head for years and years. . . . When she was 18, I did go back and discovered that that had been a lie . . . "

She described finding her daughter, living in Ottawa five minutes away from her own home. "I found her without the help of anyone but myself and good search methods. I should not have had to do that. This was my child by blood. I wanted to know if she was all right. I did not want to muscle in on her adoptive family. She had a wonderful adoptive family. She had wonderful siblings and good parents. But she also had my three other children as her full siblings and I wanted her to have the right to say 'I don't want to know you,' or 'I do want to know you,' whichever she wanted. Knowing my daughter now for 12 years has been the joy of my life."

Patricia McCarron, an adoptee who had been reunited with her birth mother ten years earlier, pointed out that even if the legislature was to pass the bill and adoptees get their original birth certificates, those adoptees would still have to decide to search for their birth parents. It wouldn't give them anything but the information.

I personally sat on my birth mother's name for 13 years. For that period of time, all I needed was the name: For a lot of people just getting a name is very important.

I am a product of sexual assault. My birth mother was not properly introduced to my birth father. What can I say? Fifty percent of my genealogy is gone forever. I will never know. However, [my birth mother] was more than happy to have contact with me.

Some members questioned McCarron about confidentiality. They approached it from every angle. "Could it not be that for some birth mothers, going forward and filing a [contact] veto would, from their viewpoint, be making a disclosure?" Parsons asked.

McCarron countered that it was simply a disclosure to the adoption disclosure registry, not to the adoptee. When Parsons responded that the woman could still fear that once she told the government, it would be out there, on record, McCarron sharply reminded him that the government already had the birth mother's file. That's how the adoption was facilitated in the first place. The mothers "had to go through a court system. There was a judge who signed the adoption order."

Parsons's questions upset a lot of people in the committee room. Many of them subsequently sent letters to Liberal leader Dalton McGuinty, complaining that Parsons was speaking for the Liberal caucus at the hearing without knowing the facts. I am happy to say, though, that Parsons—unlike many others—came to the hearings with an open mind, and he eventually came to support adoption disclosure reform.

Holly Kramer addressed directly the "apparent concern [about] the identity of so-called putative fathers." She told the legislature that the name or information about a biological father on an original birth certificate couldn't be there unless "he signed the document at the time."

Moreover, she said, "adopted persons cannot make any claim on their birth parents' estates unless the adoptee is specifically named in the will. Although concerns about allegations of paternity or claims respecting inheritance are unfounded, they may fuel some of the resistance to change."

Natalie Proctor Servant of Bastard Nation opposed the concept of allowing a contact veto at all, saying it stigmatized people involved in adoption. The group recommended instead legislation that offered a contact preference, which would have no fines attached and would allow parties to indicate if they wanted to be contacted and, if so, their preferred method of contact. Servant made the point that a contact veto was not needed because the vast majority of people who found each other did not make unwanted contact, and if they did, antistalking and antiharassment laws already existed to deal with it.

Members of the committee were able to ask questions of the deputants. This is where the real reason for the vehement opposition of some middle-aged men became clear. After Nicki Weiss spoke with compassion and wisdom as a parent who had adopted two sons at birth, Progressive Conservative Wayne Wettlaufer had this question for her: "There are some people here from my generation. We got married in the 50's and 60's, and there was at that time a habit of spouses saying to one another, 'Are you a virgin?' Whether or not you were, the answer was always yes." (Progressive Conservative Ted Chudleigh laughingly threw in from the sidelines, "Especially the guy.")

"I can see instances," continued Wettlaufer, "where the male spouse would say, I don't want to know if I've got any kids running around out there, and the female doesn't want to acknowledge it to him for fear of the damage that can be done to the relationship. Comment?"

Weiss gave a great answer:

I think lying and lack of information are more damaging than the truth. It's like saying, if your marriage is shaky, "Let's ignore our issues. Hopefully, they'll go away and our marriage will get better." From my experience, that doesn't happen. I could understand where people would be reluctant to open up the skeletons of the past, but I'm sure the relationship would be improved by greater truth.

Wettlaufer then asked: "What about those instances like we saw recently in Toronto where the father, who has long remained hidden, suddenly leaves himself wide open to a lawsuit?" Wettlaufer was referring to the case against then Toronto mayor Mel Lastman, a successful businessman who had a longstanding relationship with a woman outside his marriage. This woman gave birth to and raised two boys on her own. The sons said they grew up in poverty, and as adults, they launched a lawsuit claiming they had a right to some of Lastman's fortune.

This was a strange example to use, given that these children were raised by their biological mother, who always knew who their father was. But it served its purpose in revealing a fundamental fear of some middle-aged men, even if clumsily expressed. In their youth, they had been sowing their wild oats and may have, secretly or unknowingly, fathered children. They feared that opening up adoption records would leave them vulnerable to that proverbial knock on the door by someone exclaiming, *Hi, Daddy*.

Many concerns were expressed, but everyone had a fair opportunity to air their views and the hearings ended on a positive note. The committee met again on December 5, 2001, to begin final deliberations before returning the bill to the legislature for third-reading debate and a final vote.

Now things began to unravel. Progressive Conservative Garfield Dunlop began the proceedings on an ominous note by reading a letter into the record from government house leader Norm Sterling. Sterling, who had opposed disclosure reform all along, started by thanking everyone for their input on the bill ("particularly Ms Churley") and then, after outlining the usual concerns, he added a new one: security. Post 9/11, the Ontario government had vowed to do its bit by tightening rules around access to birth certificates. And now, the government was invoking this measure to squelch adoption disclosure reform. Then other government members expressed serious concerns without offering any remedies.

Upon hearing this, I felt a jolt of anger run through me. I had visions of jumping out of my seat and accosting him. In private conversations with Sterling, I was never able to discern why he was so adamantly opposed to disclosure reform. He did not demonstrate any interest in reading current information; he just stuck resolutely to his outdated views.

I forced myself to stay calm and to remember where this move was coming from. He, and a few other hardliners in his party, were determined to stop this bill from passing. And they were getting nervous, because they knew that a large majority on all sides of the house supported it.

Members of the adoption community were stunned by this brazen tactic. They sent letters chastising Sterling for turning the war on terrorism into a war on adoptees and biological parents who just wanted to exercise their right to access their own information. The adoption community was accustomed to being considered bastards and sluts and second-class citizens, but using us as pawns like this was just unspeakable.

Hundreds of angry letters were sent taking Sterling to task for what was viewed as a careless and contemptible misuse of concerns around combating terrorism. Sterling conveniently ignored a simple point— the records were being made available to those directly concerned, not to the general public. Even though the government had introduced this new concern, it did not propose any amendments to the bill before the committee's vote. When the committee nonetheless voted unanimously for the bill, I knew what the government's strategy was and I knew we were cooked. This was a death sentence for the bill. The government had decided to let the bill pass at committee, but to never call it for third reading and a final vote in the house.

My heart was pounding and I could barely contain myself. But I forced myself to remain calm, as I remembered how far we had come and that a significant majority on all sides of the legislature supported the bill. There was still hope.

On December 6, 2001, the bill was reported back to the house by committee chair Steve Gilchrist with some minor amendments. The Speaker ordered that it be put on the agenda for third reading. The *Toronto Star* published a supportive editorial on December 9 entitled "Time to Open Adoption Records," which drew a phenomenal response. The paper received more letters to the editor on adoption disclosure reform that week than on any other topic, as it announced with the heading "We got mail: This week topic Adoption on top of list." But as I had feared, the Progressive Conservatives didn't call the bill, even though the lobbying was fierce and I put pressure on them in the legislature almost every day.

On December 13, the house adjourned; it was to reconvene on March 18, 2002, but the schedule was delayed when Mike Harris resigned as premier. The Progressive Conservatives held a leadership convention on April 15, 2002, at which Ernie Eves was elected party leader and became premier. He won the by-election that was called for May 2, so that he had a seat when the house was finally reconvened on May 9.

During this period, I was becoming deeply involved in NDP politics at the federal level. I was among the people who in early 2002 began organizing Jack Layton's campaign for a run at the leadership of the party. Word was out that Alexa McDonough would soon be stepping aside. And indeed, the position came open in June of that year when McDonough announced she was stepping down and that a new federal leader would be chosen in January 2003.

I was honoured and thrilled when Jack asked me to be his national campaign chair. That year I spent every spare moment working with my co-chairs across the country, building his profile and raising money for the campaign. Our hard work paid off when on January 25, 2003, Jack Layton was declared winner of the leadership race after the first ballot.

Meanwhile, when the legislature resumed in May 2002, there was no sign that Bill 77 would be any sort of a priority for the Progressive Conservative government. Yet we had come so far—by now the bill had majority support in the legislature; it had gone through the committee stage and had actually passed second reading. We stepped up the pressure on the government to call it for third reading and a final vote. And we now had even more powerful ammunition to help our cause.

In July, a study by two university researchers—Charlene Miall of McMaster University and Karen March of Carleton University—showed that 75 percent of Canadians supported open adoption records, a number that roughly corresponded to the percentage of members in the Ontario legislature who supported my bill.

Philip Wyatt, chief of genetics at North York General Hospital, who strongly endorsed Bill 77, had held a news conference with us in May at Queen's Park. Dr. Wyatt said that science had identified more than 2,500 inheritable diseases, and that the current law made it impossible for many adoptees to take informed preventative action.

I frequently see patients—perhaps every month, perhaps every two weeks—in their 40s or 50s who are dying of a serious disease that they passed on to their children. But they cannot find their children. And their children, therefore, will die of the same disease their parents do because we cannot contact them to bring early treatment and diagnosis. That, I suspect, is occurring on a regular basis for adults.

We learned at the committee hearings that this was indeed occurring—lives were being lost and people were suffering unnecessarily because they were unable to get health information about their biological families. Kariann Ford, for example, suffered from a rare kidney disease that she passed on to her three children. Critical medical information was in her files, which had been passed on by her birth mother when she was sixteen years old but never given to her.

COAR put out pamphlets emphasizing that adoptees were not able to answer the simple questions that medical researchers asked to help identify people who might be genetically disposed to cancer. Has anyone in your family had more than one type of cancer? Has more than one person in your family had the same type of cancer? Has anyone in your family developed cancer before the age of forty-five? The pamphlets ended with a simple plea: "Save a life. 'Yes' to Bill 77."

We continued to pressure the government to call for a vote. I made statements in the house and raised the issue with Premier Eves in question period as well as privately, and I was very encouraged by his reaction. Eves was remarkably accessible. One day I chased him down on his way to his office after question period. When his aides tried to come between us, he stepped aside and walked me to a quiet corner, where he assured me he was in favour of passing my bill and would do what he could.

The adoption community, tasting success, swung into action. Hundreds of letters of support came pouring in to the premier, to ministers, and to house leaders. People made appointments to meet with

their representatives. We put out press releases and held press conferences. I wrote to all members of the house with relevant information.

On October 7, 2002, COAR staged a protest on the lawn at Queen's Park. Mothers dressed in black walked in a circle, pushing empty baby carriages and holding placards demanding a vote on Bill 77. Progressive Conservative MPP Marilyn

Rally on the legislative grounds in support of Bill 77, October 2002.

Mushinski, Liberal house leader Dwight Duncan, and New Democrat Gilles Bisson spoke at the rally. We read out the names of people in all three parties who supported Bill 77, including Progressive Conservatives Elizabeth Witmer and Garfield Dunlop, and Liberals Dalton McGuinty, Leona Dombrowsky, Maria Bountrogianni, Mike Colle, and Dave Levac. The entire NDP caucus supported the bill. In fact, at this point, only a small minority of Progressive Conservatives and Liberals opposed it, but they were determined to stall the vote. We were getting more and more positive media attention. In November, the *Ottawa Sun* published a story by Lisa Lisle called "It's a Motherhood Issue" and the *Toronto Star* published one by Patti Gower and Margaret Philp titled "A mother's need to know."

Still, I could not get the government to call Bill 77. On November 26, members from the adoption community filled the visitors' gallery at Queen's Park for question period to witness me ask Premier Eves if he supported calling the bill for third reading and a final vote. Our hopes soared—he said *yes*.

The next day, the *Toronto Star* ran a story by Caroline Mallan headlined "Eves backs free vote on adoption bill." The story said that "Eves did not make any promises, and hinted that the bill's passage would be subject to the usual last-minute deal-making that accompanies the end of the session," but it quoted him as backing a free vote because he believed "issues such as [this] don't have any place in partisan politics." The story also quoted me as saying I was "encouraged that the Premier has waded in."

This was the best news we had had in a long time, but we were uneasy when the premier said that Bill 77 would be one of the bills on the horse-trading block at the end of the sitting. We'd been there before. Nonetheless, I wasn't overly concerned. There was no reason to believe that the legislature would be prorogued, which meant that if it did not pass before the Christmas recess, the bill would keep its place on the order paper and I could pick up where I'd left off when the session resumed.

But then I got word from our house leader, Peter Kormos, that the government planned to recess the legislature a bit earlier than expected, on December 12, with a return of March 17, 2003. This meant less time to get Bill 77 dealt with, but even worse, there were credible rumours that the government was planning to prorogue the session at some point and return in the spring with a throne speech and a new legislative agenda.

Having come so close, we were devastated by this news. The usual shenanigans that precede prorogation played out, even though at this point it was technically a simple adjournment and not the official end of the session. There were late-night sittings and haggling between the government and opposition over passing selected government bills with minimum debate, and opposition party battles to preserve their private members' bills.

We had two days. On December 11, I repeatedly tried to get Bill 77 called for third reading and a vote, right until the stroke of midnight when the session ended. Every chance, I was on my feet asking for unanimous consent to have it called, but each time consent was denied by government members. I even tried to turn a debate on a Progressive Conservative bill on regulating puppy mills to stop cruelty to animals into a discussion on stopping cruelty to adoptees and their birth mothers. In the meantime, the government happily allowed many of its own private members' bills to be called. The night ended with my bill still on the order paper.

The next night, December 12, was my last chance. The closed-door meetings between the house leaders continued and negotiations were getting ugly. And my bill was not called before the legislature recessed. Mine was one of only two private members' bills that did not get passed that night. Our house leader supposedly had a deal with the

Liberal house leader that would see us stick together in support of calling all of our private members' bills. I felt hurt and betrayed when that deal was broken. Let me tell you, there was quite a ruckus on the floor of the legislature. I was furious with the Progressive Conservatives but also with the official Opposition Liberals, because I believed they had thrown me under the bus in order to get their bills through.

Upset and exhausted, I went to my office and banged out a press release that aptly reflects my fury and frustration:

Churley's Adoption Bill Stymied by Tories and Liberals

The Progressive Conservative Government has dashed hope of gaining a much-needed overhaul of Ontario's adoption law, says New Democrat MPP Marilyn Churley. The Tories have prevented Churley's Bill 77 to improve access to records for adoptees and birth parents from going to a crucial vote that would have finally made it law after three years of trying.... The two other parties last night worked together to allow a Liberal bill to pass along with the four other Progressive Conservative private members bills.... She said Liberals promised to help the NDP use delaying tactics last night to keep the promise of negotiation alive today, but they caved in to the government to get their own bills through. The Toronto–Danforth MPP met with adoptees and birth mothers today and pledged to keep fighting. "There were some tears, but there was also anger and renewed resolve. This is not over—we will never give up," Churley said. "My bill will be back, but in the meantime, people are becoming ill and some are dying because they do not have access to their medical histories," she said. "It's hard to stomach Conservatives once again preventing the adoption community from winning this badly-needed and widely supported update to Ontario's antiquated adoption laws while finding time to debate and vote on their own members bills."

As predicted, on March 12, 2003, the government quietly pro-rogued the legislature by order-in-council, without resuming the session. The legislative agenda was wiped clean, and the Eves government scheduled a throne speech for April 30.

Democracy in action! Here we had a piece of legislation that over 75 percent of MPPs supported, a study showing that 75 percent of Canadians supported adoption openness, the premier of the province supporting a free vote on the issue—but a small minority was still able to stop it from going forward.

We had come so close, but Bill 77 was dead.

NINETEEN

LAST STAND

OUR FOURTH AND FIFTH attempts to pass adoption disclosure reform bills presented unanticipated obstacles. On May 5, 2003, I introduced Bill 16. By now, Newfoundland and Labrador had joined British Columbia in reforming its adoption disclosure laws. Ontario, once a leader in this area, was falling behind.

The heading on the press release I put out on May 14, the day before second reading was to take place, read "Four Times Lucky." However, I didn't really feel very optimistic. I knew I had become a thorn in the government's side, and the thought of my introducing yet another bill seemed to send shudders down most everyone's spine.

Sure enough, shortly after the release went out, I was summoned to a meeting with Brenda Elliott, the minister of community and social services, and her parliamentary assistant, Wayne Wettlaufer. It was a useless encounter. Question period had already begun, and they were watching the proceedings on TV. Elliott bluntly stated that her government would support my bill only if I amended it to make it apply only to new adoptions. She cited the privacy commissioner as backup.

Her eyes were glued to the TV, and she was paying scant attention to anything I had to say. Despite that, I patiently explained that updating adoption disclosure legislation was all about opening historical records to those whom they most concerned. Most adoptions today were already open, so her proposal didn't make sense.

I quickly realized that it made no difference what I said. I strode over to the TV, turned it down, and snapped: "I can't believe you called me in here to dismantle the very essence of legislation I've been trying to get passed for years.

"Go to hell," I said as I walked out, gently closing the door behind me. I was fuming, and I was worried about what she might do to try to stop me.

Bill 16 received second reading on May 15; the vote was forty-one in favour and fourteen against. Given that the contents were the same as Bill 77, which had been through committee hearings, there was no need to send this bill to committee. I made the case that, given the majority support for the bill among all parties and the public, it should be immediately called for third reading and a final vote. Based on the votes the bill had just received, the government knew it would pass into law if it was called. To stall for time, they sent it to the Standing Committee on Justice and Social Policy.

What followed can only be described as an act of sabotage by the Progressive Conservative government. While I was arguing for a speeded up process for Bill 16, the government had Wettlaufer introduce a separate private member's bill—Bill 60—that if passed would set the cause of open adoption records back several decades. Wettlaufer's bill would not be retroactive, and it proposed to make unlawful any searches by adoptees or biological parents outside of the adoption disclosure registry. Parties who undertook such searches would be subject to fines of up to a hundred thousand dollars. This would mean that people could no longer legally solicit the help of groups like Parent Finders or search on their own for their adopted children or birth parents.

We had wondered what Elliott would do to stop my bill. The government was going to try to get this monstrosity passed so they could say they had acted on the issue and make it go away. It passed second reading by one vote, the deciding vote cast by the Speaker, who traditionally votes in the manner that allows a bill to proceed to the next stage.

With Wettlaufer's Bill 60 sent to a committee hearing, along with my Bill 16, the CCNM, COAR, and Parent Finders sprang into action. They had to. The consequences of allowing Bill 60 to be passed into law would be dire. MPPs were bombarded with emails, letters, and news releases. I issued a news release on June 12, 2003, calling Bill 60 a "cruel hoax" and "irresponsible and absolutely reprehensible."

The campaign worked, to an extent. Bill 60 quietly slipped off the government's radar and didn't proceed further. Neither, however, did Bill 16.

Bill 14, my fifth and final attempt to initiate adoption disclosure reform, came after Eves's government was replaced by the Liberal government of Dalton McGuinty following the October 2, 2003, provincial election.

Unfortunately, the New Democratic Party was essentially collateral damage of the voters' haste to get rid of the last vestiges of former premier Mike Harris's so-called Common Sense Revolution. Liberal candidates warned that if votes were split between Liberal and New Democratic candidates, Progressive Conservatives would wind up coming up the middle in many ridings to win the election. Voters responded to this plea for strategic voting, and the NDP wound up on the short end. I still won my riding by a large margin, but the party received just 12.6 percent of the popular vote and was reduced to seven seats, one fewer than is needed for official party status in the legislature.

The NDP would not have been in this position if, in 1995, when Mike Harris had reduced the number of seats in the legislature from

134 to 103, he had proportionally reduced the number needed for a political party to achieve party status. With the reduced number of members in the house, based on the average requirement across the country, that number should have been reduced to five.

Without official status, New Democrats were considered to be Independent members without party affiliation. We were afforded much-reduced office and support services, and we lost our caucus budget. Our opportunities to participate in question period and debates were greatly diminished, and when we rose to speak in the house, the Speaker referred to us by our names only, with no party designation. Even Howard Hampton was not announced by his official title as leader of the New Democratic Party. He was now just the member from Rainy River.

This shunning was too much. We believed that Ontarians, who had elected an NDP government in the 1990s, surely did not regard the NDP as some sort of "unofficial" party. And what with my plans to introduce another adoption disclosure bill, and with a lot to say on many matters of public importance, I was not content to forego my party affiliation. The Liberals were toying with us; they seemed happy to see us relegated to a lesser status and refused to compromise. One day I was complaining about the situation to Richard Mackie, then the Queen's Park correspondent for *The Globe and Mail*, and he joked, off-handily, that we should consider adding "NDP" to our legal names.

I recognized instantly that this was a brilliant idea. It might just get our fight the publicity that it needed. Living up to my reputation as the queen of stunts, I raced out of Mackie's office and down the halls to fill in a change-of-name application, wrote a cheque to cover the cost, and put out a news release. The media descended. TV, radio, and print reporters followed me as I strode, application in hand, to the Registrar General's Office to make it official.

The story caught fire. I was legally changing my name to Marilyn Churley-NDP. Once passed, each time my name was officially called in the legislature—whether for a recorded vote or to recognize me as a speaker—the words "Marilyn Churley-NDP" would ring out. In the meantime, although it wasn't official yet, my letterhead and signature were changed to reflect my new name. People loved it. Everywhere I went people called out, "How are you, Ms Churley-NDP."

All the while, there were backroom negotiations on the official status issue between the Liberals and NDP house leader Peter Kormos and deputy house leader Gilles Bisson. And I was engaged in productive behind-the-scenes talks with Liberal party stalwart Greg Sorbara, with whom I'd always had a respectful working relationship; he said he believed we were being treated unfairly. I know these discussions helped us reach a deal, but I also believe that my stunt helped move things along. It drew the public's attention to the NDP's position, and the press began to portray the Liberals as mean-spirited.

Soon after my name change, a deal was reached and the government agreed that the NDP should receive funding for more staff, as well as a regular turn to speak during debates and in question period. The issue became moot a few months later when Andrea Horwath (who would later become party leader) won a by-election in Hamilton, bringing the NDP caucus to eight members and returning us to official party status. I quietly withdrew my name change application.

Bill 14 was introduced on December 4, 2003. I had in my hands a copy of a letter Dalton McGuinty wrote to COAR when he was leader of the official Opposition. In the letter, he said he had always "voted in favour of the proposed changes to adoption disclosure procedures" and he believed that "in the majority of cases, both adult adoptees and birth parents who have given their children up for adoption should be allowed access to their records. In my view, it is a question of human rights."

Now McGuinty was premier. Based on his clearly stated support for reform, I urged him to back up his words with action and bring forward a government bill. But rather than take anything for granted, I once more carefully prepared an information package for every MPP, including a covering letter describing the bill and outlining the history of attempts to reform adoption disclosure. I attempted to dispel the main myths and described the reform that had already occurred in so many other jurisdictions. I was also pleased to include a copy of the letter Premier McGuinty had written while in opposition.

The adoption community, so experienced now in lobbying and preparing for debate, rallied again. They wrote press releases and began to inform new MPPs about the issue. With a new potentially supportive government in place, we had to make sure that cabinet was fully briefed and brought onside. We even had a new development: in May 2003, while we in Ontario were wrangling over Wettlaufer's Bill 16 and my Bill 60, Ralph Klein's government in Alberta passed legislation to reform its adoption disclosure laws, and the records were to be officially opened to the public in November 2004. Ontario was now lagging behind British Columbia, Newfoundland and Labrador, Alberta, and seventeen countries.

The media's support for opening up adoption records kept growing. *The Globe and Mail,* for example, published a story by Murray Campbell titled "Painful Memories Drive Churley's Adoption Bill."

COAR had a positive meeting with Sandra Pupatello, the minister of community and social services, and shortly after that, I met with her as well. I was encouraged that she brought two staff members who asked many good questions and took copious notes. Her senior policy assistant Gurpreet Malhotra in particular was a quick study, and he became the key staffer in Pupatello's office who did a tremendous amount of work on the bill. Pupatello's biggest concern centred on providing privacy to those who wished to remain anonymous.

When I explained that the contact veto actually added a protection that didn't exist under the present system, she was very positive about moving forward. She asked for background information, which was certainly no problem. We provided reams of it in short order, and I kept her private phone number on my speed dial. Although no promises were made, it looked as if Pupatello was interested in bringing in a government bill, in which case my private member's bill would be superfluous. A bill brought in by the Liberal majority government would be assured of passing.

Shortly after we met, Pupatello indicated that the government indeed intended to bring forward legislation to reform adoption disclosure. She introduced Bill 183 for first reading on March 29, 2005. With this development, we decided to withdraw my private member's bill. Surely, now, we were on the verge of success.

PART IV

NO MORE
SECRETS

TWENTY

FATHER AND SON

N JUNE 2004, as I was fighting for my final private member's bill, Billy and Milena got married. Both of Billy's families attended the ceremony and the reception afterwards. The four parents had met before, all proudly attending his graduation in 1998. Now, on this occasion, all the brothers and sisters, nephews and nieces were able to connect. At the wedding, Billy's father, Chris, and I sat in the front-row aisle right across from his adoptive parents, Bram and Helen, and Billy went out of his way to be attentive and kind to all four of us.

It had taken some doing to get to this point. In the early days of our reunion, Billy and I had spent countless hours together and things moved along very quickly. I'd told him quite a bit about the circumstances of his conception and birth, including why I gave him up for adoption and some not-so-kind details about his father. He wanted to know everything—he soaked it all up. And things sort of spilled out; I wasn't very circumspect about what I revealed.

So one day I asked him a rather big question: Did he want to meet his father? He looked uncertain and said he wanted to think about it.

Billy and Milena at their wedding with both sets of Billy's parents, June 2004.

With Chris and our son on Billy's wedding day. Don't we look happy!

The next time we got together, he looked me straight in the eye and said, "Yeah, I would really like to meet Chris—I'd like to see what kind of man he turned out to be."

I got it. And it brought tears to my eyes.

Adopted people who want to know about their origins are not looking to replace their adoptive parents. They just want to know who they are and whom they look like. They also want to know what they are likely to be like when they get older. And, of course, there are family medical histories to consider. Those of us who grow up in our biological families take these things for granted. You look in the mirror and curse your Uncle Bob's big nose. Your mother tells you that you sound just like Aunt Nora when you laugh. You know your grandmother and your aunt had breast cancer so you take precautions and get screened early.

I had completely lost track of Chris. The last time I'd seen him we had a terse and unhappy conversation. It was at a party in Toronto sometime after I returned from New York, a year or so after I had given birth. He asked me what had happened to the baby. I told him it was a boy, that he'd been adopted, and that I didn't know where he was. Chris expressed shock that I had given up the baby and suggested that I try to get him back so he could take care of him. It was such a preposterous and tactless thing to say. I walked away in disgust and I hadn't seen him since.

Now I found myself searching for him. I hardly knew where to begin. He had a very common last name, and I didn't know much about his family.

I inadvertently got a direct lead to Chris at a political gathering. After the Ontario NDP suffered its spectacular loss to the Harris-led Progressive Conservatives in the 1995 election, Bob Rae announced his resignation effective June 22, 1996. My friend Frances Lankin, then the member for the riding adjacent to mine, Beaches–Woodbine (now Beaches–East York), was the first to announce her intention to run for the leadership. I proudly endorsed her and joined her nomination committee. Shortly thereafter, Tony Silipo, Peter Kormos, and Howard Hampton signed up. The race was on.

New Democrats from all over Ontario came to the convention in Hamilton, at which Hampton was declared the winner. At a party afterwards with the Lankin camp, I found myself talking to a man from Ottawa who knew some of the same people I had known in that city. As we were reminiscing, I told him the story of my son, which led to my explaining that I was looking for his father. I asked if he had any idea where I might find him.

It turned out that not only had he stayed in touch with Chris, but he also had a current number where Chris could be reached! He promised to send it to me after he got back to Ottawa.

A few days after I arrived home from the convention, my telephone rang. I could not believe my ears when Chris identified himself. His old friend had done what I had expressly asked him not to do—he had called Chris and given him the news, man to man. I didn't know Chris at all anymore, and it was important to me to have control over how this information was revealed to him. I was upset and angry, but it was too late for any of that. Here we were, having the conversation.

Chris's voice was shaking. He was excited but also traumatized by the news. We talked for more than an hour as I told him how I'd found Billy and what he was like.

Then he dropped a bombshell. He said that he was concerned that the child was not his and wondered if it might all be a hoax in an attempt to get money out of him. I was insulted to my core, but I forced myself to coolly explain that once a child was relinquished for adoption, you not only lost all parental privileges and rights, but you were also relieved of all responsibilities. I wanted to slam down the phone and never speak to him again, but I had to focus on the main goal—my son wanted to meet his father. I was going to do whatever it took to make that happen.

Several days passed. Chris called back and asked me if we would be willing to have blood samples taken for DNA tests. That gave me pause. Could I ask my son to do this, so that his father would accept him? I agreed because I had no choice. I still had only one goal. But it took me a while before I worked up the nerve to ask him.

When I finally did tentatively tell Billy about Chris's request, he seemed to be taken aback, as I suspected he might be, and said he needed some time to think about it. Even though he was overjoyed that I had found his biological father, it took him a while to decide what to do. In December he wrote to me saying that he was willing to go ahead with a DNA test. After working out the details with Chris, I made an appointment at a clinic close to home, and the samples were sent to British Columbia for testing. We were told it would take at least four weeks before the results were ready, and that they would be relayed to Chris. He would be the first to know.

I knew Chris was the father. Of course, he was the father. There was no way that he couldn't be the father. But still, weird thoughts started fluttering in my mind like little birds. We all get nervous waiting for important test results. What would I do if I were wrong?

On February 26, 1997, Chris called me with the results. His voice broke as he confirmed that he was Billy's father. After all our nervousness, we rejoiced together and began planning for him to come to Toronto to meet his son. He would also now be able to tell his daughters that they had a brother.

Chris had written a letter to me before he was confirmed as the father. Understandably he was traumatized by the whole situation. He wrote that he was feeling nervous but relieved that Billy was willing to go through with the DNA test so we would all know for sure about paternity. He also wrote that whatever the outcome, he was experiencing "surf quality waves of shame and guilt" and that he was finding it hard to forgive himself for being such a jerk.

A few weeks later, I picked up Chris at the airport. As we careened along the expressway back to my place, we got into an intense and emotional conversation. My pent-up anger and hurt spilled out, as I told him about the loneliness and terror of the childbirth and the anguish of losing my son. I caught myself; this was not a good time to talk about it.

Just as I was about to change the subject, Chris apologized for letting me down and causing me so much pain. But in his next breath, he said something that took the sweetness out of the moment. When we had first talked on the phone, he'd told me that he wanted to be sure it was his child. But now he explained why he had doubts. He told me some of his friends had convinced him that I was one of those women who got pregnant to trap a man into marriage and that he was the one I'd picked to marry. After all I had been through, this was too much. It's a wonder I didn't pull off the road and strangle him with my bare hands.

We did, however, arrive home in one piece and have a fantastic gathering at my house. My daughter, Astra, and my grandson, James, joined us for meals. We talked and talked and got to know each other, and Billy spent a lot of time alone with his father.

We found out that Chris's father had been a famous documentary filmmaker in the 1950s and '60s. He was now in his eighties and dying. Chris had not yet told his mother about Billy and didn't want to during this difficult time. Nevertheless, he wanted Billy to see his grandfather before it was too late, so he took Billy to Ottawa and managed to sneak him into his father's room for a brief visit. Shortly afterwards, Chris told his mother about his son, and she welcomed Billy with open arms. Billy would join the family at his grandfather's funeral a few months later.

Billy visited Chris in British Columbia and Chris came back to Toronto. Sometimes they met at his grandmother's house in Ottawa. She accepted Billy completely and joyfully as her grandson, and treated him lovingly from day one. She died a few years after they met, but during that short time, they became very close. Chris's eldest daughter, Billy's half-sister, wrote a beautiful letter to Astra and me, and shortly after that she came to Toronto for a visit. Astra went out to British Columbia to visit them. And so it went.

When Billy came back from his first visit with Chris in 1997 with photographs in hand, I understood completely why he needed to meet his biological family and why most adoptees want so badly to

know where they came from. He handed
me a black-and-white photo that featured

Billy and Chris finally meet.

about thirty young men squatting in that familiar way boys' sports
teams pose for a camera. The small faces looked very much alike to me.

"That's my father's high school soccer team. Can you tell which
one is Chris?" Billy asked eagerly.

I scoured the faces, desperately hoping I would pick the right one.
I finally pointed to the face that most reminded me of my distant memory of Chris as a young man. Billy's face fell. Wrong guy. He pointed
to a little face and said, "I can't believe you couldn't tell. At that age, he
looks just like me!" His own face glowed with satisfaction.

That was so important, so dear to him; to have a picture of a man,
his father, who looked just like him. That's why we needed to change
Ontario's laws. So it would be easier for adoptees to find their birth
parents, and to give them the chance to experience the joy that Billy
had finally found.

TWENTY-ONE

THE COMMISSIONER
AND THE LAWYER

T HAD BEEN a long haul from my first private member's bill in 1998 till the McGuinty Liberals introduced Bill 183 in 2005. The public now had a better understanding of the issue, and many media outlets were supportive of reforming the laws. Even the minority of MPPs who stuck to their outmoded ideas knew that the time had come. After being barraged with mail from the CCNM, COAR, Parent Finders, and hundreds of adoptees and birth mothers, they gave up the fight for a non-retroactive bill. Instead, opponents now pushed for the inclusion of a disclosure veto.

The government bill wasn't perfect. My bills would have made it mandatory for biological parents to file updated medical information, even if they wanted a contact veto in their files. The Liberal bill only encouraged them to provide that information. And in what appeared to be a cost-saving move, the Liberals proposed eliminating government assistance with searches and reunions, as well as counselling services. We were concerned that private agencies would rush in to fill the void, making searches unaffordable to low-income people. As well, private agencies would have less access to information than a government agency did, particularly in terms of the non-identifying information that was held in files owned by Children's Aid societies.

But at least we had a bill, and one that was backed by a majority government. The bill was assured of going to committee hearings, where we would have a chance to propose amendments.

The debate now was between those who wanted the legislation to provide full access to all original birth and adoption information to both adult adoptees and birth parents, and those who wanted one or the other party to be able to file a veto that would prevent the disclosure of their information. There was general acceptance on allowing a no-contact order to be registered, but the fight over an information disclosure veto proved to be pitched and protracted. Bill 183 did not initially include a disclosure veto, and I—and many others—felt strongly that none should be added.

Most modern adoptions are open; the parties usually have some form of contact with each other. A disclosure veto that pertained to previous adoptions would create two classes of adoptees—those who had access to their personal information and histories, and a small minority who did not. The same could be said for birth parents; most of them would know where their children were, but some would have no idea. While British Columbia, Newfoundland and Labrador, and Alberta included disclosure vetoes in their legislation, we now had convincing data from other countries that showed no evidence of any problems. In fact, in June 2005, after careful study, Western Australia removed the disclosure veto from its adoption legislature.

At the 2005 hearings, arguments on privacy were put forward by two formidable opponents of unrestricted information disclosure— Ann Cavoukian, Ontario's privacy commissioner, and human rights lawyer Clayton Ruby. I was somewhat shaken when I saw Ruby sitting next to the commissioner. He is deservedly respected as a brilliant and fearless lawyer who takes on a variety of progressive cases, and on most issues, we were on the same side. I had often been a guest in his home, where he and his wife graciously hosted fundraisers for environmental and human rights causes. It was difficult to find myself on a different side of this issue, particularly as it was so important to me.

Cavoukian issued relentless public criticisms following the introduction of the bill. Ruby threatened a constitutional challenge on behalf of an adoptee who did not want his information disclosed to any searching birth parent. This caused many MPPs who had previously supported my bills to get cold feet. As well, Cavoukian's dramatic performance in the committee hearings and Ruby's commanding presence at news conferences garnered a lot of press. The media became increasingly critical of fully opening past adoption records without allowing parties to register disclosure vetoes.

Those of us fighting against the veto argued that if something is right then all must benefit—not just those born after a certain date or only under certain conditions. Disclosure vetoes create two classes of adoptees and violate the UN Convention that every person has the right to their identity. The experience of other jurisdictions with disclosure vetoes showed that, whether they are applied against the biological parents or adopted adults, they are hurtful and punitive and prevent medical information from being transmitted. The Ontario Association of Children's Aid Societies, the real experts in this area, wholeheartedly supported retroactivity and were against a disclosure veto. We just could not back down on this.

Committee hearings, which opened on May 18, 2005, got off to a rocky start. The Progressive Conservatives were not happy to see the bill introduced and proceeded to hold up the start of the deputations. Things got ugly. Nasty, off-the-record insults flew back and forth between Liberal and Progressive Conservative members. I pleaded with them to allow the proceeding to begin and I was joined in this effort by Kathleen Wynne, the Liberal point person on the committee. Eventually, Liberal Mario Racco, the committee chair, got things back on track and the committee hearings got underway. Given his difficult position, Racco remained remarkably calm and did his best to be fair to everyone.

Cavoukian was the first to speak. Intense and influential, she was well respected by the media and the public, and she presented a real problem for us. I tied to catch her eye, but she never once looked in my direction throughout her deputation.

She was trembling with emotion as she began, saying that although she supported more openness in adoption disclosure, she could not support making disclosure retroactive to people who thought they had a right to privacy and who thought that their information held by the adoption registry would never be accessed. She said she'd received hundreds of letters, emails, and calls from people who were frightened by the bill.

"Here is a small sampling of their voices. I have to read this," Cavoukian said to a transfixed crowd in the hearing room.

"I am one of the young girls who thought they were safe," Cavoukian read. "When I signed the adoption papers some 35 years ago, I was promised in a courtroom that my identity would be protected and that no identifying information about me would ever be released. I feel betrayed by the system."

Cavoukian read another message: "You must vigorously defend my right to privacy. I am so angry I'm shaking, but I can't voice my anger since I feel I must remain silent about my past. How unfair to all of us who must remain 'voiceless' that this will be retroactive."

Another letter, then another, and another. After reading each letter, she slammed it on the table. And then, this:

Another birth mother who wanted to remain anonymous, who was raped at the age of 17, became pregnant and gave her child up for adoption: "I don't wish to give my name or have anyone seek me out. I don't wish to see the child. I don't know who the man was who raped me. I can't tell them anything about that man. That was way back in the 1960s.... I was promised that my name wouldn't be disclosed... I would feel just ultimately betrayed.... I'm afraid I would just simply go in the garage, and shut the garage door, and block the exhaust in my car, and end my life over this."

Cavoukian finally stopped reading and, in an emotional voice, said, "It breaks my heart reading those things to you."

She then delivered a short lecture on defining privacy. "The most important aspect of privacy is control: personal control over the uses of your own personal information.... Freedom of choice is at the heart of privacy. Access to one's own personal information is certainly an important component of privacy, but it is not the primary consideration. Control relating to the uses of your own information is key."

If it was about control of your own information, we thought Cavoukian was missing a critical point. Adoptees had no freedom of choice; they didn't even have access to their own information. Someone had decided when they were born that they would be denied their personal information and they would never be able to gain access to it. It was *their* information, and they had no control over it.

Cavoukian's appearance at the committee was powerful. Clearly there were people who supported her view, and she felt that it was her role to make their voices heard. But we knew that she was speaking for a small number of people, and her performance seemed out of proportion. In fact, I was told by Karen Lynn that she, along with Grand and Rowney, unsuccessfully attempted to meet with the privacy commissioner to discuss this very matter. Eventually they were given a meeting with her one of her staff, who, according to Lynn, informed them that the privacy commissioner had received about 150 letters concerning adoption disclosure. About half of those were against the disclosure veto. Lynn said angrily to me after the meeting, "So, the entire adoption community who supported open adoption records was being held hostage by the privacy commissioner and her approximately seventy-five letters of opposition."

Cavoukian's office sent out several press releases, including one on March 29 that said: "I keep thinking of the young girls who gave a baby up for adoption 20 years ago thinking they were safe, and never thinking that a government would reveal their secrets." This came after we explained repeatedly that the ability for people to find each other had grown over the years and that, in fact, the bill's contact veto would offer a protection that did not currently exist.

At the hearings, Clayton Ruby represented Denbigh Patton, an adoptee who opposed any bill that didn't include a disclosure veto. Patton spoke respectfully of those who favoured the bill, but made it clear that he would direct Ruby to challenge it in court if it passed as it was. He said that, as an adoptee, he alone should be able to decide whether he would, as he put it, "expose myself to my birth mother, my birth father and other relatives." Ruby cited privacy rights embedded in Canada's Charter of Rights and Freedoms, as well as an Alberta case that upheld a non-disclosure provision in that province's adoption information legislation.

We worried that the threat of a court challenge from such a powerful legal voice would scare the government into amending the bill. But the purpose of the bill was to end discrimination against adoptees and birth parents, and we remained determined not to back down on the veto. This led to trouble. Between Cavoukian's demands for a disclosure veto and Ruby's threat of a lawsuit, we began losing media support. Newspaper editorials that advocated a disclosure veto began sprouting—even in the *Toronto Star*, which we had counted on to be on our side. Previously supportive members from all parties were getting nervous.

The hearings heard from several people who adeptly put forward the case for full and open disclosure of all adoption information so that all Ontarians might have access to their personal histories. I wish I could put every person's deputation into this book. Their frustration, their pain, their joy, their anger, their compassion all came pouring out so eloquently. They were speaking from their own realities and from their own experiences.

Monica Byrne and Holly Kramer, representatives of two branches of Parent Finders—which by that time had assisted more than twelve hundred people in contacting and reuniting with birth relatives—addressed issues raised by the privacy commissioner. Holly Kramer said that in her years of experience in these matters, birth relatives contact each other without violating each other's privacy. "You can contact birth families. You can contact birth mothers. We do it on a daily basis. You do not publish the information on the front pages of the *Toronto Star*. You are doing it one on one, discreetly. . . . It is not a matter of making the information known to the public." She told the committee that, in fact, her own adoption order from the 1960s had her full birth name on it. "There was no confidentiality," she said. "My birth mother had a very rare German name. It was not a hard thing to find her."

Monica Byrne confronted the fears Cavoukian had given voice to in her testimony.

I'm the birth mother [Cavoukian] is defending so eloquently. I gave birth to a child in Ontario in 1966, so I came from those days of secrecy, privacy, and all that other stuff that was associated with being a birth mother then. I was forced through the system to have to crawl and grovel to get information and find my daughter on my own.... I married her father. I have three other children, her full siblings. We had a very positive reunion.... I like her mother; her mother likes me. We are not in competition. That girl is both our daughters. It's normal and okay and we're mature about it.

Byrne challenged the "red herrings and fear mongering" that she said Cavoukian had promulgated. And she brought the issue down to basics.

No one wants his washing out on the public lawn. Everyone would like some level of privacy, but most people would like to know what happened to their children.... In England, records have been opened since 1976. It's okay, folks. It really works. We can do it. We've made pathology out of this. This is a very normal process. These were only babies; it wasn't the plague.

She also challenged the notion that mothers had somehow been promised confidentiality by the government. "I was never offered confidentiality; I had it imposed upon me...I never signed anything."

Byrne and others also reminded the committee that with the contact veto provision, which was definitely included in Bill 183, there would be a remedy in law to prevent people who didn't want to meet their birth relative from receiving the mythical knock at the door. But adoptees would still be able to gain access to their own personal information, and parents could find out what had happened to their children.

Although most of the people who spoke to the committee supported the legislation, the London Coalition of Adoptive Families favoured more openness but wanted protection for children who were taken from their biological parents because they had been abused and made wards of the Crown. This concern was taken up by the Progressive Conservative members on the committee and, as a result, the government brought in an amendment that would allow adoptees and birth parents to come before a special committee to ask for exemptions if they could prove that it was necessary to prevent sexual harm or significant physical or emotional harm. But this solution enraged the Progressive Conservative members, who argued that it was unfair to make people come before a committee to state their case on such a personal and sensitive subject. This provision led to bitter debate in committee and, later, in the legislature.

As the hearings went on, I couldn't help but reflect on my own situation. I wasn't trying to speak for anyone else, but I had personal experience as a mother who saw and signed legal documents when I relinquished my child, and I had also served as registrar general of Ontario. I felt I could better assess the reality than could a privacy commissioner or even a human rights lawyer, both of whom I had always respected. I had no doubt that some women were afraid of being "found out" by their families or being located by their grown children, and that some had been verbally told that their secrets would never be divulged. But they were the minority, and furthermore, they would be better protected under the new legislation. I constantly reminded everyone that the bill would not legislate the right to a relationship, but would allow only for the right to access personal information and history.

The issue is about heartbreak and tragedy. We were trying to deal with the culture of a time that caused so much harm. We didn't, however, want the debate to be reduced to the rights of a birth mother who had a child as a result of rape or incest, versus the rights of an adult adoptee to know where they came from. Biological parents and adoptees have a right not to be contacted, but all people, no matter what the circumstances of their birth, have a right to their own personal information.

We were greatly concerned by the privacy commissioner's reading of the note from the elderly woman who threatened suicide. It was compelling and chilling, but it was an approach we had chosen not to use. I had letters from adoptees who were experiencing brutal emotional problems after trying unsuccessfully to find out about their roots. Many were depressed and fearful, and some were, indeed, suicidal. Studies indicate that the suicide rate among adoptees is higher than in the general population.

Karen Lynn, in her deputation in support of Bill 77, stated that she knew of one member of the CCNM who threw herself under a truck after attending family court. The woman had had to watch her baby being held by a social worker while she was forced by her parents to testify that she was relinquishing her baby of her own free will. Luckily, she was not seriously hurt. The truck driver crawled under the truck and held her as she cried and told him her story.

But we didn't use this information in our campaigns. We did not want to create the disturbing competitive quagmire of who is most at risk. Surrendering a child is a deeply personal, emotionally wrenching decision. I received hundreds of heartbreaking letters and saw many lives that were shattered by the secrecy. Adoptees lived in fear over questions about their health for which they couldn't find answers, wondering what they might pass on to their own children. There were many mothers (and some fathers as well) in their seventies and eighties who longed in their hearts to find their children before they died.

I had found my son by piecing together non-identifying information that was available, such as where the adoptive parents had lived, and by the kinds of ordinary sleuthing—both low- and high-tech— that we can all use to find things out. As it turned out, my son had always known my name; it was on the adoption order given to his adoptive parents. This brings up the question: If privacy was so important, what about my privacy? What had given the government the right in 1968 to give my name to the people who had adopted my child? (Not that I minded, but they were trying to have it both ways.) And as a former registrar general, I can categorically say that no evidence supports the claims that legal contracts ever provided for confidentiality.

It wouldn't have taken my son very long to find me, if he had decided to do so. There was only one Churley listed in the Toronto phone book—M. Churley. And in the 1990s my signature was on a certificate in virtually every elevator in Ontario. (There's even a song written about it by a fine Toronto musician, Kurt Swinghammer, called "The Signature of Marilyn Churley.") Billy might have done that kind of searching. As it turned out, I looked for him first.

My reunion with my son has been nothing but a blessing for both of us. As Bill 183 wound its way through the legislative process, I could only hope that it would become easier for so many others to have the opportunity to find each other. And perhaps to be able to experience what we had.

TWENTY-TWO

VICTORY!

N EARLY MAY 2005, just before the hearings on Bill 183 began, I was invited to give a keynote in Washington at an international women's conference. I shared the stage with Hillary Rodham Clinton—a highlight of my years in political life. We had a chance to chat privately, and I found her to be intense and focused but extremely friendly, with an easy sense of humour. She spoke of her failed health-care plan and her determination to keep working on it; I spoke of my frustration in trying to reform adoption disclosure legislation. We shared a passion for the rights of adopted people: she had worked to improve America's adoption and foster care systems to provide safe, loving homes for children in need. She was keenly interested to learn about the health implications of children growing up with no knowledge of their genetic backgrounds.

I got back to work on the adoption bill as soon as I returned with new energy and determination. But by the time public hearings finished on May 19 and the committee began clause-by-clause consideration of Bill 183, we—the many supporters of adoption disclosure reform—were drained and fearful. The concerns expressed by the privacy commissioner, the hype generated by the Progressive Conservative opposition, and the resulting negative press had had an impact.

We recommended amendments that would have restored what we had proposed in my earlier bills—a provision making it mandatory for birth parents to file updated medical information, even if they also filed a no-contact order; and commitments by the government to assist with searches and reunions and to provide counselling on request. The Liberal majority on the committee did not accept these amendments. But rather than risk losing the bill altogether, we kept quiet about our reservations.

When the bill came back into the legislature for third reading, Progressive Conservative leader John Tory (now mayor of Toronto) hounded the government daily during question period. He repeatedly conjured up the image of a now seventy-five-year-old rape victim living in fear that the child she had borne would suddenly show up at her door and cause her to relive her experience. Sandra Pupatello and I spoke to Tory many times, pointing out the absurdity of using this argument to counter sensible legislation. The bill's no-contact provision did not even allow such a scenario. But that story provided a powerful image, and Tory—though I felt he was rather uncomfortable using it—was under pressure from the hardliners in his caucus to keep it up. Tory was also influenced by Cavoukian. He stated during third reading debate that although he had voted for the bill on second reading, he'd changed his mind after the privacy commissioner telephoned him to discuss some of her concerns.

Pupatello and I stayed in close touch during this rough period, and I carried some of the freight for her. Her strength and courage were admirable. She was under tremendous pressure from some of her Liberal colleagues. I could even feel a few of my caucus members getting anxious, what with the daily conjuring of a story about an elderly woman being forced to relive a rape experience. Who could blame them?

I wished they could all have been at the committee hearings to witness Graig Stott's remarkable deputation. A self-described happily reunited adult adoptee and a psychotherapist, he had been working for more than ten years with clients dealing with the damage caused by secretive adoption legislation. He spoke directly about his own experience.

My own search and reunion has not been without its painful hurdles for my mother, for my adoptive family and for myself. My mother's story around my conception and subsequent relinquishment was hard for me to hear and come to terms with. She is very much like the elderly birth mothers that Ms. Cavoukian spoke of yesterday. My mother was a victim of a rape that resulted in my birth. My mother was terrified about letting me into her life and opening up those secret wounds, but, at the age of 75, and in her own time, she eventually did, and in her own time and in her own way, she chooses to share more and more of herself and her story with others in her life. She wasn't forcibly exposed to the world.

My mother, at 78, has shared stories with me she has never shared with anyone else: stories of my conception, her pregnancy and my birth. My presence in her life today has helped her move away from living her remaining years in unresolved grief and fear. She is no longer a victim.

Her presence in my life has alleviated a degree of daily, moment-to-moment fear and anxiety that I assumed everyone felt and that I thought was normal.

The weight lifted from our shoulders and hearts and the healing that has reverberated throughout both my families is nothing short of miraculous. This is what healing is. It can be painful and frightening. It takes guts and courage. As is evidenced with my own mother, I am not suggesting we force people to deal with issues they are not inter-ested in or not yet ready to face. This would be arrogant, disrespectful and counterproductive. When the parties are ready, they can move forward, or not, in a timely and appropriate manner. It's their choice.

In early June, the pressure on the minister and the premier took its toll. Pupatello announced that the final vote on Bill 183 would not take place before the summer recess; instead, it would be delayed until the fall. We were crestfallen. We could see the whole thing slip-ping away again. The Progressive Conservatives would use the summer to whip up public sentiment against the bill. And some truly outrageous things were being written in the press. Adam Radwanski, then a columnist and editorial writer at the *National Post*, wrote that the legislation, and my efforts over the years to reform adoption information disclosure, had the potential to encourage a future teen-aged woman who didn't want to keep her child to have an abortion rather than carry the baby, give it up for adoption, and then face "the possibility of her life being torn apart when she's 36 and the kid turns up on her doorstep."

It didn't seem as if the debate could get any lower. I kept a Ben Franklin quote in mind as I responded to his article. "If passion drives, let reason hold the reins."

Yes, I had a huge passion for this issue. But I always knew passion alone was not going to win this war. My weapons were hard, reliable facts.

The writer's appalling suggestion that more unmarried pregnant women would terminate their pregnancies with the passage of the bill suggests that he was unaware that most adoptions today are already open. That is, information is exchanged and, in many cases, some sort of relationship is maintained. As a result, young mothers making the difficult decision to relinquish their children now are comforted by the knowledge that they will not lose track of their children completely. And the column completely ignored the legislation's mechanism to legally prevent the kind of contact that the writer described, that it would recognize adoptees' and birth mothers' right to privacy.

After I calmed down, I wrote a letter to the editor, part of which was published by the *National Post*, in which I reiterated the main points. I thought we had made these points sufficiently over the years, but they were now being driven off the front pages by the conjuring of theoretical scenarios that did not represent how people dealt with real things in the real world.

"This bill is not a search-and-reunion statute," I wrote.

This legislation, in keeping with the bills I have brought forward, is about the right to personal information, not a relationship or even contact. Because of the circumstances of their birth, adoptees for decades have been denied a right that all other adults enjoy—the right to know their birth information and history. . . . It is ridiculous to suggest that all individuals involved in adoptions want to be reunited, and that all reunions go seamlessly and joyously. I have heard from hundreds of adoptees expressing they do not want contact with their biological parents and vice versa, as well as from those who made contact and were disappointed by the outcome. But every one of those say they are still glad to know where they come from and the circumstances of their birth so that they can move on with their lives.

We were thankful that the *National Post* later published a balanced article by Heather Sokoloff called "A Fight over Identity."

In September, Cavoukian issued a news release that actually helped our cause. In what she titled an Adoption Identification Alert to birth parents, she finally acknowledged a fact that we had been asserting all along. Historically, until at least the second half of 1969, all Ontario adoption orders showed the adoptee's birth name (the mother's legal name at the time she signed the adoption papers). After 1969, it was hit and miss. Some adopted babies had their surnames blacked out or replaced by a number, while others had surnames included. This backed up our argument that many adoptees, especially those who were adopted before 1970, likely knew their mothers' last names and could, if they chose, use this information to help locate them. The law as it stood did not have a contact veto option. The new bill would allow adoptees to have access to their own personal information, but also force them by law to abide by a birth parent's no-contact order.

When the legislature reconvened in September, we went back to work to build support for Bill 183. Even though it was a government bill, I was one of the go-to people for the media, so I was often debating and rebutting Cavoukian or her deputy on the retroactivity of the legislation. This constant back and forth with the commissioner was stressful, but it had to be done.

On September 14, I held a news conference with Karen Lynn and Michael Grand of COAR, and with Kilauren Gibb, the daughter Joni Mitchell had given up for adoption. Sitting next to Gibb, I couldn't help but feel things had come full circle. It was reading about her reunion with her mother that had prompted me to go public with my story in 1997. And that had led to my political fight to change the disclosure law.

Gibb, who looks a lot like her famous mother, was nervous before the news conference began. But she was brilliant when she spoke about the joy and completeness she felt when she finally reunited with her birth parents after years of searching that had left her feeling empty and lost. Although she declined to speak for her, she said she believed that Mitchell would support the legislation. After months of despair, the positive publicity from the news conference was just the lift we needed.

The debate finally came to an end. On October 31, Pupatello moved third and final reading of the bill. The Speaker formally stated in a loud, clear voice: "Ms. Pupatello has moved third reading of Bill 183, an act respecting the disclosure of information and records to adopted persons and birth parents. Is it the pleasure of the House that the motion carry?"

A booming "no" emanated from the Progressive Conservative benches, automatically triggering a recorded vote that, by prior agreement, would be held the next day.

So here it was, November 1, 2005, the big day. I could hardly contain my excitement.

The Speaker read out the motion, then signalled for all members of the house to be called in within five minutes. At 2:28 p.m., with everyone seated, the clerk announced: "All those in favour will please rise one at a time and be recognized by the clerk." I could feel all eyes on me, even though, as sponsor of the bill, Minister Pupatello was the

Adoption disclosure activists celebrate the passing of Bill 183 at the home of CCNM member and reunited mother Barb Estabrooks (standing, far right).

first to stand. After her, the rest of the Liberal caucus rose to be counted. When the Liberals were finished voting, I was the first of the New Democrats to stand to vote. I had tears streaming down my face as I bowed to the Speaker. And when I made that affirmative nod, the lid came off the place. It erupted for several minutes in loud and joyous cheers and hoots. After things calmed down, each of my fellow New Democrats stood one by one to vote yes.

The Speaker then asked for all those opposed to stand, and every Progressive Conservative member who was present rose to vote no. A few of them were not in the chamber for the vote, most notably John Baird, who had always been supportive of reform. Later, Baird told me he wanted to come in and vote in favour, but felt he couldn't break with his caucus. That's why he opted to stay away.

Then came the final tally, declared by Claude DesRosiers, clerk of the assembly: "The ayes are 68; the nays are 19. I declare the motion carried."

I was overcome by emotion. After more than twenty-five years, fairness was coming at last to adoptees and their birth parents.

Members of the house, even those who had voted against the bill, were on their feet, pounding on their legislature desks, and applauding wildly. Pupatello, in an uncharacteristic move by a government minister, crossed the floor and shook my hand to congratulate me on the passing of her own bill! NDP leader Howard Hampton held my arm up in the air like a referee declaring the winner of a boxing match. My colleagues cheered and came over to hug me.

The visitors in the gallery, which was full of people connected to adoption whose hopes had been raised and dashed so many times over the years, were cheering and weeping. Best of all, my son sat only a few feet away from me. And he was grinning from ear to ear.

TWENTY-THREE

VICTORY DELAYED

OW I WISH I could say that that was the end of the story.
Immediately after the bill passed, Clayton Ruby announced
with great fanfare that he would launch a constitutional challenge on behalf of three adoptees and a biological father who
were opposed to the new law because it didn't allow people
to file information disclosure vetoes. This meant the government
would not proclaim the bill until the court ruled. The legislation was
in limbo while the old law remained in effect.

In late 2005, I stepped down as the MPP for Toronto–Danforth
to run federally in the riding of Beaches–East York, the riding next
to Jack Layton's. It meant a lot to me to be working with Jack again.
I ran against a long-time Liberal incumbent, and although I came
close in the January 2006 vote, and again in 2008, I fell short at the
same time that Jack's NDP increased its seat total and popular vote.
Even though I was out of politics, Jack and I remained close and we
continued to spend time together when he was in Toronto.

COAR, at this time, was granted intervenor status for the court case.
The group supported the government's position that an information
disclosure veto would negate the primary purposes of the legislation,
which were to make sure that all Ontarians, regardless of when or

under what circumstances they were born, would have full access to their own birth information, and that all birth mothers could find out what had happened to their children. COAR was a strictly volunteer organization that had no money, but two prestigious law firms offered pro bono services. And supporters began donating to COAR for the case. Two days after it sent an appeal to its email list, the group raised more than twelve thousand dollars from many parts of Canada and the world. This allowed COAR to hire a lawyer, Ivan Whitehall. When the court case was heard on June 25 and 26, 2007, I attended the proceedings with representatives from COAR and other activists.

The case started well for us. The presiding judge stated, "I'm not ready to buy those three words: 'right to privacy,'" and said that the lawyers mounting the constitutional challenge on behalf of three adoptees and a birth father "have the tougher job." We were elated to hear this. However, in the end, the judge would side with the challengers, writing that the legislation breached the privacy provisions granted by the Charter of Rights of Freedoms. "The rights of the searching adoptees or birth parents to the disclosure of confidential adoption information, although important and heart-felt, are not protected by Section 7 or any other provision of the Charter," wrote Justice Belobaba in his Reasons for Judgment, which was released on September 19, 2007.

The government could appeal the Superior Court decision. Or it could remedy the situation by including a disclosure veto in the legislation to comply with the Charter of Rights and Freedoms.

We had a tough decision to make. I met with the adoption community leaders who had worked so hard to get the bill passed without a disclosure veto—Holly Kramer, Karen Lynn, Michael Grand, and Wendy Rowney—and they in turn talked to others in COAR and Parent Finders. After reading the decision carefully, they believed the government stood a good chance of winning an appeal. But the process could take years—years that would come at the expense of putting in place a new disclosure law. They decided that three-quarters of a loaf was better than no loaf at all. With mixed feelings, they relayed their position to the minister.

On November 14, the Ontario government announced that it would not appeal the court decision and that it would instead introduce a new bill. In order to comply with the court decision, the bill would include both a disclosure veto and a contact veto. Bill 12 was introduced on December 10, 2007, and passed into law on May 14, 2008, with little fanfare. It would come into effect a year later, in order to give sufficient notice to those affected. On June 1, 2009, Ontario's new, hard-fought adoption disclosure law—Access to Adoption Records Act, 2008—came into effect. At long last, previously sealed adoption records would be open for adopted people aged eighteen and over; and for birth parents named on the registration of live birth, once their adopted children turned nineteen.

Several months later, the Ontario government began releasing birth certificates to adoptees and biological parents. By this time, my son was such a big part of my life that seeing the documents I'd craved for so many years no longer seemed that important. I didn't get around to applying for them until September 2011.

As it happens, this was soon after the death of my dear friend Jack Layton. When Jack was diagnosed with prostate cancer in December 2010, he was resolute and confident that he would beat it, and he continued to work hard through it all. I often drove him to events in Toronto, and although he appeared to be in pain, I never heard him complain.

A few months after his very successful May 2011 election campaign, through which the NDP became Canada's official Opposition, Jack announced that he had developed a secondary cancer and would step aside as Opposition leader. I visited him about two weeks before he died. Walking into the room, I braced myself for the worst—and it was bad. Jack sat in a reclining chair, looking so very fragile. I thought I might drop to the floor in anguish. But Jack saved me. His blue eyes, which looked huge in his thin face, lit up when he saw me, and he smiled broadly.

"Marilyn, I am so glad to see you," he said in a weak voice, but with all the enthusiasm that was Jack. His indelible spirit leapt out at me; for a few minutes, it was like old times. Except, of course, it wasn't.

We didn't talk directly about his impending death. We spoke of our families, especially—and proudly—of our grandchildren. He wanted to hear about my recent road trip back to Labrador with my two sisters. We talked of our friendship and of all the things we had worked on together, and of the fun we'd had. We spoke of his legacy and all that he'd accomplished, and the kind words and gifts he'd received from Canadians in the previous difficult months.

As I was leaving, Jack struggled to stand with the help of his daughter and a friend. "Come here," he said to me. I walked toward him and asked him if we could hug. "Gently," he said. We carefully put our arms around each other and our eyes met. No words were spoken. We both knew this was our goodbye.

Jack, who died on August 22, 2011, supported all of my efforts, but especially my adoption bills. He knew how much getting those laws changed meant to me, and no matter how hectic his political life was, he would take the time to ask me how it was going. And when success finally came, he was thrilled for me. As soon as he returned from Ottawa he took me out to celebrate—over a glass of red wine, of course—and on that evening of celebration in late 2005, he encouraged me to write a book about my adoption experiences.

When I finally did apply for the documents relating to Billy's birth and adoption, I ran into unexpected problems. Something silly I had done in my past came back to haunt me. I filled in the application and sent it to Thunder Bay with a cheque. To my surprise, a couple of weeks later, I received a letter from the Registrar General's Office informing me that a piece of information didn't match the birth registration I had completed at the time. Specifically they asked me to verify my place of birth. I had written Old Perlican, Newfoundland, and it occurred to me that at the time of the birth I may have put down my place of birth as Happy Valley, Labrador—the place I think of as home. I corrected the error, mailed in the application again, and waited.

And waited. Eventually another letter arrived stating that the place of birth still didn't match. I was puzzled and didn't quite know what to do next. Then one morning as I was getting ready for work, I received a phone call from an employee of the Registrar General's Office. After she verified that I was indeed Marilyn Churley, she asked me my place of birth. I tried Old Perlican and then I tried Happy Valley. Neither worked. She hesitated a bit and then she asked, "Have you ever been to England?"

Then it hit me. "Oh my God," I asked, "did I write down that I was from England?"

I had. I suddenly remembered having written that on the birth registration. That's the story I'd told Perry, and I couldn't risk the social worker knowing the truth in case she said something to him.

With that glitch worked out, I finally received a copy of the original birth registration, the registered adoption order, and a copy of the substituted birth registration. It was surreal looking at the statement of birth that I had filled in and signed more than forty years before— documents that had a profound impact on my life and my son's life.

That moment brought it all full circle. I was drawn back to the unbearable pain that came with being a pregnant teen in 1968, a time when hiding things and living a lie often seemed like a safer idea than telling people the truth.

We can be glad that those secrets have been unlocked, to the joy of a great many people, by the laws of Ontario.

TWENTY-FOUR

REFLECTIONS

T HAS BEEN many years since this journey began when, in 1968, I gave birth to a baby boy and, feeling that I had no other option, relinquished him to strangers. You have read about how my life was affected by losing, and then, years later, finding my lost child. But other people were profoundly affected as well.

My mother was one of them.

I've thought a lot about her over the years of writing this book. I regretted that I never asked her what it was like for her when, at the same age as I became pregnant, she found out she was going to have a baby. I had learned not to ask her questions about her life; when I did try, I had always felt rebuffed. But now I really wanted to know. What was the birth like? How did she feel about marrying my father?

After my father died in 2001, my mother moved in with my brother Max and his family in Winnipeg, where she lived out the rest of her days surrounded by love. Determined to get answers to my questions, I planned to go and spend some time alone with her. But just before I got there, she became ill. I ended up spending almost every waking hour with her in a hospital for two weeks, watching her health deteriorate rapidly.

As she became weaker, she talked more and more about her child-hood—about her mother dying in childbirth when she was only four years old; about her eight brothers and sisters (one of whom was her twin), who all died either at birth or as small children. She spoke longingly about never getting to know them, and wondered if finally she would be reunited with them. She told stories about her easygoing, loving father, Fred, who had died of a stroke many years before. She spoke about her dearly beloved stepmother, whom she called Aunt Lucy. She talked of how good her Aunt Lucy was to her and of the friends and cousins with whom she roamed the hills of Bay de Verde as a child. She didn't talk much about her marriage and her children, and I decided to let her abide in the world she wanted to be in. She died shortly after that on July 24, 2006, and now I'll never know.

But I do know that she welcomed my son—her eldest grandson—with open arms. She'd asked for a picture, which she propped up along with photos of her other grandchildren in her home in Carbonear. This surprised me. I thought she would be reluctant to have to tell her friends who he was. She told me she didn't care anymore—he was her grandson and that was all that mattered.

My mother was much beloved by her grandchildren. All of them, including Billy, came to Newfoundland for her funeral. Billy had a chance to meet his extended family and, on that sad but close occasion, he was lovingly brought into the circle. I thank my mother for that.

My daughter was intensely affected by the arrival of a big brother in her life. We still talk about that monumental discovery of hers and how it long dominated her thoughts and feelings. But when the reun-ion finally happened, I was so wrapped up in the excitement of connecting with my long-lost son that I didn't pay enough attention to what was going on with her. In retrospect I see that the early years of our reunion must have been very difficult for her, and I wish I could do that part over again.

When I found her brother, she was a new young mother herself, and when Billy came to live with me over a summer break, my daughter developed a debilitating headache that lasted for months. She went to several doctors, but it took a psychiatrist to determine that the headache was a manifestation of having to deal with the new kid on the block who was taking up all Mom's attention. She had grown up as an only child; here was the lost boy who had come and stolen my heart away.

Now they call each other sister and brother. Over the years, they have grown very close. Billy has a sister and brother he grew up with and whom he loves very much, just as he does his adoptive parents. Those are the people he bonded with, and they are his family. Yet, there is also a unique bond between my daughter and my son.

Chris ended up on Salt Spring Island, British Columbia, where he married the love of his life; together, they raised three beautiful children. He didn't go through life grieving for and wondering what had happened to his son, because in his mind he didn't believe the child I was carrying was his. But since I found him and he has connected with Billy, he has been feeling sorry and guilty. He told me he feels what he did was the greatest mistake of his life.

He recently wrote the following to me:

After your soul shattering experience and my dreadful mistake in thinking myself into denial about being the dad, the outcome is good, thanks to his dear, wonderful parents. I deeply regret having played the arch villain in this story. But your experience via the book will no doubt help others. So many have had this kind of thing happen back in the dark days of the 60's when shame and guilt ruled the issue around sexuality and out of marriage pregnancies. I confess I am in a black box of guilt still about how I reacted, and failed to react to your tearful assertion that I fathered the child we both created.

Chris described being in a state of mental wilderness at the time and desperately seeking guidance and help. He said he had dropped out of the world and jumped into an all-out "spiritual trip," adopting "the charismatic ex-monk" (Mathew) as his guru, and I didn't fit into that.

I told Chris I forgave him a long time ago and it is time to let go of the guilt and be as good a father he can be to his son.

Billy is now married to a lovely woman named Milena, and I have a terrific little grandson, Tristan, who is a big part of my life. That family is part of my family, and we do the same things that other families do together.

I asked Billy how being adopted and then found affected his life. He said it was complicated and hard to define. When I found him, he said that he had been told he was adopted when he was a small child and he felt that it had no impact on him. Now he says the truth is that he doesn't really know how any of it has affected him—both being adopted and being found—but he knows that it has.

He is happy to have us all in his life. He is glad to know about his background and says it is one he can "be damn proud of." He laughs and says that it sure makes Christmas more complicated.

As for me, politics is truly over now. After Jack died, there was a by-election for his federal seat of Toronto–Danforth, and at the urging of a host of former constituents, I almost ran. The support was tremendous and it was very tempting, but I decided to stay put to be able to continue to enjoy spending time with my family. A significant and special portion of that time is spent with five-year-old Tristan, the beloved child who has relinked the chain that was broken so many years ago.

I have my son in my life and I feel whole. But I still can't look at his childhood pictures or talk about the reunion without bursting into tears. I can remember my own harrowing experience and hear heartbreaking stories about other women's pregnancies, the loneliness of their confinement, the terror of the birth, and the numbing process of giving the baby up without crying. In a way, what happened to me happened to "someone else"—a teenaged girl who may still be lurking in me but is safely locked away. I don't think I'll ever let her out, although writing this book is giving her a little room to connect with the adult me.

But speaking about my reunion with my son still breaks me. For a long time I wondered why. After all, my dream had come true and my lost boy was found. But now I think I understand. I was a tough little nut—a real survivor—and as bad as things were, I got through it and was able to do well in my life. But what I really wanted was to get my baby back. After the exhilarating emotional upheavals of reunion, I was once again at the centre of that overwhelming pain, that sadness and longing. I realized it would never completely go away, that I would never get to be the mother who raised my own son. Nothing in the world will change that.

But that's the way it is. After all the pain and suffering, what counts is that I have my son in my life. And because of the legislation reform, a lot of other mothers have their adult children in their lives, too. Even some who were initially afraid that the legal changes might open up wounds best left alone.

One such woman is the vivacious Suzanne Van Bommel, who worked for Liberal MPP Steve Peters. She approached me in an agitated state one day at Queen's Park to tell me about a baby boy she had placed for adoption when she was a teen. She hadn't told her husband and children, and she was terrified that if Bill 77 passed, her secret might be revealed. That bill, in 2001, was our closest call of the five bills I introduced. She begged me to withdraw it, but I could see through her fear that she loved her son and longed to know what had happened to him. I gently reminded her that if the bill passed, she would have more privacy protection, not less.

I lost touch with Suzanne for a long time. Then recently, I received this message from her on Facebook.

> Hi Marilyn, I just wanted to drop you a quick note and update. I have been reunited with my son who will be turning 27 this August. We could not be happier. I remember so clearly my fear when you first introduced your private member's bill. I am glad I am no longer that scared and frightened person. Oftentimes at Queen's Park we get caught up in the game that is politics and I wonder if anything some of us did makes a difference. You have made a difference. This touches so many lives and has made me a complete person. Thank you for being brave enough to do this and thank you for starting the process that helped me find my son.

Yes, Suzanne, we did make a difference.

LOOKING AHEAD

HE BATTLE TO reform adoption disclosure laws in Ontario was a long and protracted one, with many twists and turns. We were largely successful, but we didn't get everything we wanted. As of publication, adoption records have been opened up to adoptees and biological parents in the Canadian jurisdictions of Alberta, British Columbia, Newfoundland and Labrador, Ontario, and the Yukon. Manitoba, though it will not release identifying information without consent, provides a number of services that make it easier for adoptees and birth relatives to find each other. The government has announced that it will bring in new disclosure legislation in June 2015. New Brunswick completed public consultations on reforming disclosure laws in 2014 and plans to proceed with opening up adoption records, although no date has been provided as of the publication of this book. In the United States, Alabama, Alaska, Colorado, Kansas, Maine, New Hampshire, Ohio, and Oregon have opened their records. Connecticut, Delaware, Illinois, Massachusetts, Montana, Oklahoma, Tennessee, Vermont, and Washington allow partial or restricted access; New Jersey will lift restrictions in 2017.

Adoption disclosure organizations in Canada and the United States continue to work hard to reform disclosure laws. Many want to know about the doggedness, unity, and mutual support that we used in the Ontario fight. We called it the three-legged stool: a respected and dedicated legislator (with very thick skin) on the inside; a tough, cohesive, and knowledgeable coalition on the outside; and at least a few sympathetic media voices. What started out as an adoptees' rights movement grew into a strong coalition of adoptees, birth mothers (and some fathers), and adoptive parents who were able to put aside their differences and support each other. As a result, we became a formidable force in fighting for change. Members of the Coalition for Open Adoption Records, Parent Finders, and other experts now assist in many jurisdictions. Wendy Rowney, a co-founder of COAR, was deeply involved in U.S. reform as an active member of the American Adoption Congress.

Lobbying efforts in the United States have focused almost exclusively on the rights of adoptees. In Canada, we found that working together and standing up for each other creates a stronger, more cohesive lobbying effort, and also helps dispel harmful myths—about birth mothers, especially—that can get in the way of reform.

Ontario's adoption information disclosure law, which came into effect on June 1, 2009, allows adopted people eighteen and older to see their previously sealed adoption records, and allows birth parents named on the registration of live birth to see the files of their adopted children who have turned nineteen. The law allows adopted adults and biological parents to file a disclosure veto if the adoption was finalized before September 1, 2008. This prevents the release of information that identifies the person who filed the veto. If the parties are okay with having their identities released, but don't want to be contacted by the other party, they can file a contact veto.

The Ontario adoption community continues to lobby the government to address flaws in the legislation. A mandatory review of the law in 2014 was an opportunity for the government to look at the problems in the legislation and their impact on people who are searching for their adoption information. Unfortunately those concerns were not addressed, and adoption disclosure advocates are still looking for future opportunities. Outstanding issues with the Ontario law are as follows:

1. Through the information disclosure veto, a small minority of people continue to be discriminated against; they are still denied their birth information or the information concerning the whereabouts and well-being of the children they gave up for adoption. The government could add a provision that a disclosure veto must be renewed after a reasonable length of time—perhaps five years. Such a provision has been implemented in New Zealand, resulting in a decreased number of disclosure vetoes. Having to renew the veto gives people the chance to reconsider it periodically. As it stands now, the Ontario veto remains in effect until it is removed by the initiator or until the initiator dies.

2. The disclosure veto blocks all information-sharing, including of vital medical history that birth parents might be willing to share. The government argued that no one can be compelled to give their medical history, but there is no legal impediment to encouraging people to voluntarily provide this information. The government could revise the legislation so that when a disclosure veto is filed, the person would automatically be sent a form on which to provide family medical history details. If given the chance, many people would want to provide at least this kind of information to blood relatives.

3. Under the legislation, unless birth fathers signed the original birth registration, they are not allowed to access the names of their children, and adoptees have no way of getting the names of birth fathers who did not sign. If the birth registration was signed by a single mother (which was generally the case), the government

usually deleted the name of the biological father she named. This happened even if the father declared paternity at the Registrar General's Office and signed a document to that effect. In Ontario, the Children's Aid Society (under the Ministry of Children and Youth Services) retains the names of these fathers, but only the Registrar General's Office (under the Ministry of Government Services) can release them. The government could provide a mechanism to allow the transfer of information between the two ministries. To complicate matters, in some cases, the fathers' names remained on the birth registrations that the CAS sent to the registrar general. In May 2013, the Registrar General's Office went to court to stop the disclosure to adopted people of those fathers' names. The Coalition for Open Adoption Records, Parent Finders, and the Canadian Council of Natural Mothers provided submissions to the court opposing the restriction. (A decision in the case was still pending at the time this book was published.)

4. The current law does not extend beyond birth parents and adoptees. Biological siblings, grandparents, adult offspring of adoptees, and other children of deceased biological parents can't obtain identifying information about missing adoptees. The government could fix this by extending the legislation, as has been done in other jurisdictions, including Newfoundland and Labrador in 2013.

5. People born in another province but adopted in Ontario cannot receive their original birth information, nor can biological parents receive the amended names of adoptees. All provinces need to acknowledge this problem and amend their legislation to allow the information to be shared. Again, this was done in Newfoundland and Labrador's 2013 amendments.

6. The government should reinstitute an agency that helps people search for birth relatives, something it did away with when the new law came into effect. Much of the search involves government

records and, even if the government charges a user fee, it would still be more affordable to many people than the services of private investigation organizations.

7. Many adoptees have reported that they have waited up to seven years to obtain from the Children's Aid Society non-identifying information about their birth parents, and that the information was often incorrect. The government could revise the law to include standards for time limits and veracity that the CAS must meet.

RELATED ISSUES

There are several important ongoing issues relating to biological origins and identity that this book does not cover. They are been addressed by others, but I want to touch on them briefly here.

FIRST NATIONS: It is impossible to give the appropriate weight in this short summary to the treatment of First Nations in this country and the historic harm caused by government programs. The majority of Canadians are by now aware of the appalling harm caused by residential schools, but may not be as aware of a program that took First Nations children from their homes and gave them away. In 2010 an Ontario First Nations group launched a class action lawsuit against the Canadian government; shortly thereafter, they were joined by British Columbia and Saskatchewan groups. This government-sanctioned program, entitled Adopt Indian/Métis children, is known as the Sixties Scoop. An estimated twenty thousand Aboriginal children across Canada were taken from their families and adopted out to mostly white, middle-class families throughout Canada and the United States. Those affected have eloquently spoken out about the impact it had on them—the loss of their cultural identity, lost contact with their natural families, no access to their medical histories, and for status Indian children, the loss of their status. Incredibly, this shameful government policy was not discontinued until the mid-1980s. Proper records were not kept, and many adoptees will never know their biological roots.

The Canadian government launched an appeal against the lawsuit and on October 1, 2013, the Ontario Superior Court of Justice ruled that the Sixties Scoop case in Ontario could proceed as a class action. But in May 2014, the government received permission to appeal the decision granting a class action certification. The appeal was heard by Ontario's Superior Court on November 13, 2014. On December 2, the Ontario Superior Court unanimously dismissed the federal appeal, allowing the case to proceed as a class action. This will be the first known legal action testing Canada's treatment of a generation of Aboriginal children who lost their cultural identity. Marcia Brown Martel, one of the lead plaintiffs in the court case, and her lawyer called the December ruling an "unprecedented" one that "sets the standards for protecting cultural rights of all peoples."

While this legal wrangling was playing out in the courts, Canada's Aboriginal affairs ministers requested that Canada's premiers look at compensation, counselling, and repatriation for those who were affected by the Sixties Scoop. Many see the adoptions as an extension of the residential schools policy, which was designed to "take the Indian out of the child." Manitoba Aboriginal Affairs Minister Eric Robinson, a residential school survivor, said what they experienced was as or more traumatic. "In my case, at least I had other Indian boys and other Indian kids my age to be around. In the case of these kids who were adopted out, they had nobody. They were a brown face among a mass of white faces either in the United States or in foreign lands. In some ways, they had it a lot worse."

Brown Martel was taken from her family when she was four. In an article in the *Toronto Star*, she told of her adoptive mother vigorously scrubbing her with soap to get the "dirty brown colour" out of her skin. Numerous shocking stories recount the racism and abuse many of the children endured.

Now, as adults, many are trying to reunite with their birth families and communities, and some birth parents are seeking their lost children as well. This can be a difficult process complicated by cultural and identity issues, given that the children were mainly raised in white families. Several Aboriginal reunification programs across Canada have been set up to help with the search and with the emotional and psychological issues that may arise. To learn more about this issue, go to http://sixtiesscoopclaim.com.

REPRODUCTIVE TECHNOLOGY: As the fight for open adoption records is being won, it is astounding to see the same mistakes being repeated when it comes to offspring born through donor-assisted conception (DC). They are coming of age and many of them are demanding to know who their biological parents are. These adults are being treated as children by the state, just as adoptees used to be. They are forced to depend on the state and other adults to give them their own birth information.

A 2011 landmark B.C. Supreme Court ruling, in response to a case brought forward by Olivia Pratten, who wanted information about her biological father, said that the existing legislation was unconstitutional. Pratten argued that children conceived through sperm donation should have the same rights to access information about their biological fathers as children who are adopted. The judge ruled "that donor offspring share with adoptees many of the same... needs for information about biological parents, and that, even if well-intentioned, serious harm can be caused by cutting off a child from his or her biological roots."

The judge also ordered a permanent injunction against the destruction of donor records. However, the government appealed, and in 2012 the B.C. Court of Appeal threw out the earlier decision. Pratten took her case to the Supreme Court of Canada, but in May 2013, the court announced it would not hear her case, without stating why.

Pratten and her supporters, while disappointed, pointed out that this is an area that has no legislation, and as more and more women are delaying their fertility, more people are using egg donors and surrogates. The issue is not going away. In Western societies, donor-assisted conception has risen dramatically primarily because of the advancements in technology, particularly where a third party provides an embryo or sperm or eggs to allow a woman to conceive. Donor insemination, a simpler process, has been in practice much longer.

An excellent U.K. paper by Eric Blyth, Marilyn Crawshaw, Jean Haase, and Jennifer Speirs was published in 2001. The paper reviews access to genetic origin information in adoption and examines to what extent these practices may be relevant to donor-assisted conception. Throughout the United Kingdom, secrecy in adoption is now formally discredited. The paper compares adopted children and off-spring born through donor-assisted conception and concludes that there are similarities in the need to know their biological origins.

Single men and women will continue to have children through adoption and DC. Lesbian couples, gay couples, and heterosexual couples—married or not—will continue to adopt and have children through DC. The gay and lesbian community began the trend away from secrecy. In particular, the growing number of lesbian couples choosing to conceive with donor sperm led to more openness for their children and consequently for all children conceived through donor assistance. Dr. Sue Rubin, co-founder of the Ethics Practise in Berkeley, California, and chair of the identity task force at the Sperm Bank of California explains, "Early on families were counselled never to disclose the fact that they had used donor insemination. Those were primarily straight couples, and the goal was to preserve the presumption of the father's identity in the family. But as more lesbians and single women became clients, the initial reason for secrecy wasn't applicable." And, I would add, most of these couples wanted the best for their children and understood that access to their biological history was paramount to their emotional and physical well-being. The same health issues and identity issues that concern adoptees concern children who are born through DC.

Fortunately, many countries are eliminating donor anonymity, but Canada is lagging behind. The Assisted Human Reproduction Act was passed in 2004; while it provided for information registries to be set up, information could only be released if the donors gave their consent. But it is a moot point because they never were set up. Moreover, this entire section of the AHR Act was repealed in 2012 as a result of the Supreme Court of Canada badly split (4-4-1) decision regarding the challenge by the Quebec government regarding provincial versus federal jurisdiction in matters of health.

Sweden, Norway, Finland, Switzerland, Austria, the United Kingdom, the Netherlands, New Zealand, and the State of Victoria in Australia have put mandatory donor identification release in place. Several sperm banks in the United States have an "open identity" program that lets women and couples pick their donors by referencing letters and sometimes photos and videos. As well, these sperm banks will assist mothers and children of any age if they request to meet previously anonymous donors, by contacting the donor and setting up a meeting if agreement is reached. And the Donor Sibling Registry, an American non-profit organization set up in 2000, has enabled thousands of people conceived as a result of sperm, egg, or embryo donation to make mutually desired contact with others with whom they share genetic ties (that is, donors and half-siblings).

The evidence is inconclusive and conflicting as to whether ending anonymity decreases the number of donors. But for the offspring—the people who are most directly affected by donor conception—there is plenty of evidence, based on personal anecdotes, as well as on psychosocial theory and international research, that donor anonymity is not in *their* best interests.

Phyllis Creighton, a historian and ethicist, author of a 1977 book on donor insemination, and a committee member of Health Canada that helped draft legislation on assisted human reproduction, addressed adoption disclosure committee hearings on the issue. She had been thinking about these kinds of issues from an ethical viewpoint for a long time and she came squarely down on the side of openness. Reflecting on what she had learned from donor-conceived individuals through written sources and personal conversations, she made this statement at Bill 77 committee hearings on May 18, 2005:

> In my experience, people want to know where they come from and who their kith and kin are. Curiosity about where one's traits came from seems instinctive. I think one's identity and the meaning of one's life hinge on knowing one's parentage and on having a historical family framework. Knowing your history grounds you in this fast-changing, bewildering world. Roots are a need today. Witness the people searching provincial archives for their family tree. Knowing your family's genetic and medical history can also be of life-saving importance.

FOREIGN ADOPTIONS: Since reproductive choice in Canada and the rest of the Western world has become the norm and attitudes toward single parenthood are changing, international adoption has become more common. The controversial adoption of a baby from Malawi by Madonna in 2005 brought stinging criticism and made us think about the morality of taking children from poverty-stricken families. For example, on May 30, 2012, a *Globe and Mail* headline read "Profit-driven adoptions turn children into commodity." The story was about a report released by the African Child Policy Forum, which states that the number of African children adopted by foreigners has nearly tripled in the past eight years as a result of financial gain for some and lack of proper safeguards. Some parents report that they are told their children are being sponsored to go to school or taken for temporary foster care, but the children are never seen by their families again.

Human rights groups point out other ways to rescue poor children and to help their parents in villages to keep them in their own communities and in their extended families. We can push our governments to increase foreign aid, as is repeatedly promised but never done; we can support the many existing programs and aid organizations that are working to keep families together. Some of those have started programs to feed, educate, and give affection to children placed in orphanages by their parents because they were unable to afford to take care of them.

Because of my experience with relinquishing a baby partly due to a lack of resources and support, I have a great deal of sympathy for women who gave their children away to foreigners. It is useful to think about people who adopt babies in the Western world, where birth mothers are given some months to change their minds and a chance to take their babies back. These women and men describe how instantly they bond with their adopted babies and the fear and pain they feel at the thought of their babies being taken back by the birth mothers. So why would it be different for any of the impoverished women who carried their babies in their bodies, who brought them into the world and heard their first cries, who held them and fed them and were forced to give them up because of lack of choice?

I am not against foreign adoptions per se. There is evidence that in many cases adoption by affluent and loving parents from foreign countries is in the best interests of the child. I have friends who are living testimonies to that. But I believe that just as we have moved to open adoptions in most of the Western world, every effort should be made for adoptive parents to meet the birth mother and relatives and some connection be maintained with them. The birth parents should be given the option to stay in touch with the adoptive parents, and exchanges of photos and letters should be part of the adoption arrangement. This is already the practice of many adoptive parents, but more must be done to ensure that all foreign adoptions are conducted properly and lawfully.

STOLEN BABIES: In 2011, a BBC documentary revealed horrific news about the theft of possibly up to 300,000 babies in Spain. The BBC reported that the babies were given or sold to new parents, beginning under Franco's regime, and that the practice continued into the early 1990s, as newborn babies were stolen by doctors, nurses, and nuns from obstetric wards and sold to new parents. The biological parents were told their newborns had died and were given false death certificates and burial information.

As a result of those reports, more women are coming forward to tell their stories. The *National Post*'s Kathryn Blaze Carlson researched Canada's practice between the 1940s and the 1980s of coercing or forcing young unmarried women to give up their babies. In some cases, they were told that their babies were dead. She cites the 2011 book *The Traffic in Babies: Cross Border Adoption and Baby-Selling Between the United States and Canada, 1930–1972* by McMaster University professor Karen Balcom, who writes that in Nova Scotia there were "numerous examples of birth mothers who were falsely told that their children were dead so they would not interfere in adoption placements."

On November 15, 2010, the Australian Senate launched an inquiry into its former forced adoption policies and practices. The committee heard from hundreds of women, many of whom said they were coerced into signing away their children while others said their signatures were forged and that they were drugged. In a report released in March 2012, the Senate called for a national apology to the thousands of women who were forced to give up their children for adoption from the 1950s to the 1970s. Many Canadian birth mothers are demanding the federal government hold a similar public inquiry; this campaign is led by Origins Canada (www.originscanada.org).

These stories have a common theme. Children by the millions have been taken from their homes abroad, adopted domestically, stolen and sold or given away, born through donor assistance and their identities taken from them by the state. There are many reasons why children are raised by people other than their biological parents, and when that happens—for whatever reason—there are two things that really matter: that the parent or parents raise them and fulfill their needs in a loving, supportive home, and that the children know and have some connection to their biological roots.

It's the second one that that we collectively have the power to make happen. I hope that the fight we engaged in in Ontario will encourage those working on these issues keep going until they achieve victory.

RESOURCES

HOW TO APPLY FOR ADOPTION INFORMATION IN ONTARIO

For applications and details on obtaining adoption information, visit www.serviceontario.ca. The following are some general guidelines.

1. If you are adopted and at least eighteen years old, you may apply for your original birth registration. It will provide your name at birth, the then name of your biological mother, and, in some cases, the name of your biological father. You may also apply for the adoption order.
2. If you are a birth mother, you may apply for your adult child's (aged nineteen and over) amended birth registration, which will state your child's post-adoption name. You may also apply for a copy of the original birth registration.
3. Adoptees and birth parents may also apply for non-identifying information about the other parties. This information was compiled at the time of the adoption and provides background information about the birth and about the adoptive family, without names. You will receive either a summary of the information

compiled by a social worker or a copy of the original file with all identifying information removed.

4. If you are a biological father, you can get the same information the mother gets only if you are named on, and have signed, the original birth registration. All biological fathers can, however, apply for non-identifying information and can place their names in the Ontario Adoption Disclosure Registry, as can all other birth relatives. If the adoptee applies to the registry, the government will notify all parties.

5. Adoptees and biological parents can file information vetoes, contact vetoes, or notices of contact preferences. A notice of contact preference means that either party, upon filing for birth information, receives a form that is used to inform the other party about how and when contact should take place.

OTHER PROVINCES

For adoption information in other Canadian provinces and territories, visit these links:

- Alberta: Human Services
  (http://humanservices.alberta.ca/adoption/14846.html)
- British Columbia: Ministry of Children and Family Development
  (www.mcf.gov.bc.ca/adoption/info_adults.htm)
- Manitoba: Family Services
  (www.gov.mb.ca/fs/childfam/registry.html)
- New Brunswick: Services
  (www2.gnb.ca/content/gnb/en/services.html, search "post adoption disclosure")

- Newfoundland and Labrador: Service NL
  (www.servicenl.gov.nl.ca/birth/
  accessing_records_under_adoption_act)
- Northwest Territories: Health and Social Services
  (www.hss.gov.nt.ca/publications/forms/
  adoption-registry-application-information)
- Nova Scotia: Community Services
  (http://novascotia.ca/coms/families/adoption/
  AdoptionDisclosure.html)
- Nunavut: no website available, phone 867-975-5781
- Prince Edward Island: Department of Community
  Services and Seniors (www.gov.pe.ca/sss, search
  "post adoption service")
- Quebec: for information about adoptions finalized in Quebec,
  you need to know the exact Youth Centre (Centre Jeunesse)
  involved; for more information, visit Mouvement Retrouvailles
  (www.mouvement-retrouvailles.qc.ca)
- Saskatchewan: Social Services
  (www.socialservices.gov.sk.ca/adoption)
- Yukon: Health and Social Services
  (www.hss.gov.yk.ca/adoption.php)

UNITED STATES

If you are an adoptee who was born in Canada and subsequently taken
to the United States, contact the U.S. Department of Immigration for
a copy of your entry visa. This form should have your full name at birth.

There are a number of excellent U.S. websites, including the American Adoption Congress site (www.americanadoptioncongress.org),
which has links to other websites and government agencies.

INDEX

Churley, Andrew. *See* Billy

Churley, Eddie: and Billy, 112, 131–6, *136*; character and values, 31, 132; death, 137; education, 13–14, 16; employment, 14, 17; and Marilyn, *22*; marriage to Myrtis Emberley, 13–14; parenting, 19, 26, 27, 31–2, 42, 131

Churley, Edna. *See* Roberts, Edna

Churley, Fred, 18, 74, 136

Churley, Joan. *See* Cameron, Joan

Churley, Marilyn, personal. *See also* Astra; Billy: abortion attempt, 42–4; acting, 66; adoption of son, 1, 50–1, 59, 95, 108, 119–20, 134, 171, 173, 175, 188, 202, 203, 206; adoption records, 4, 80–1, 201–2; Barrie, Ontario, 49–56, 62–3; and Billy's adoptive family, 111–12, 121, 171, *172*; birth of daughter, 69, *71*; birth of son, 1, 53–4, 56, 101, 108, 171, 175, 203; boyfriends, 26–7, 33–4, 35; and Chris (Billy's father), 40–1, 45–7, 119, 171–7, *172*, 205–6; cousins, 22; and Doug, 73, 118–19, 134; early years in Happy Valley–Goose Bay, 14–33, *16, 19, 20, 22, 26, 32*; editor of school yearbook, 31; education, 20, *20*, 31, 72–3; employment before political career, 61, 64, 66, 73; feminism, 2, 29, 32, 66, 77, 78–9; first renewed contact with Billy, 95–100, *98*; goals of adoption reform efforts, 5; grandchildren, 5, 111, *120*, 121, 136, 176, 206; grandparents, 14, 21–2, 132, 204; and Jon (Astra's father), 66–9, 72; labour and childbirth, 51–3, 68–9; longing for son, 59–60, 62, 63, 72, 81, 94, 95, 96, 98, 99, 101, 113, 115–16, 118, 207; marriage to Richard Barry, 78, *79*; missed years with Billy, 117, 120, 206–7; Montreal, 67–72; New York City, 60–2; Newfoundland, 21–2, 28–9, 34, 64–5, 202, 204; nieces and nephews, 74; Ottawa, 31, 33–6, 39–42, 45–7, 173; Parent Finders, 91; and Perry (pseud.), 49–51, 54, 56, 59–66, 69–70, 202; personal response to political events, 11, 12, 105; pets, 18–19; political awakening, 36; pregnancy, 41–2, 45–52, 67, 68, 108, 134, 207; public revelation of adoption story, 105, 108–11; public speaking, 28–30; questions about son, 4, 75, 90, 97, 111; raising daughter, 71–2, 75–6; reunion with son, 4–5, 100–2, *101*, 108, 117–18, 134, 171, 188, 203, 206–7, *242*; Ryerson University, 73; search for son, 4, 81, 90–6, 187–8; secrecy about Billy, 75–6, 105, 112, 113, 114, 131–3, 202; secrecy about pregnancy, 2, 42, 44, 45, 47, 48, 52, 63, 131–2, 202; separation from infant son, 53–6, 59; sex education, 23–7; student life in Ottawa, 31, 32–6; telling family about Billy, 132–5; Toronto, 66–7, *67*, 73, 76–7; travels in Europe and North Africa, 66, 75, 114–15; use of adoption disclosure registry, 91, 95; Vancouver, 72–3; Victoria, 47–9; Withrow Public School, 77

Churley, Marilyn, political. *See also* adoption disclosure reform; individual private member's bills: activism, 76–7; amalgamation of Toronto, 107–8; antiwar movement, 66;

Ontario New Democratic Party (ONDP). *See also* individual members: 1990 election of majority government, 4, 80; amalgamation of Toronto, 105–8; government, 9–12, 80, 82, 89, 93, 105–6, 122–3, 126, 180–1; loss of official party status, 164–6; and strategic voting, 164; support for adoption disclosure reform, 123, 126, 158, 191, 196

Ontario privacy commissioner. *See* Cavoukian, Ann

Ontario Standing Committee on Social Policy, 11

Ontario Superior Court of Justice, 214

open adoption. *See under* adoption

open adoption records. *See under* records, birth and adoption

Origins Canada, 221

orphanages, 219

Ottawa. *See under* Churley, Marilyn, personal; Parent Finders

Ottawa Citizen, 109

Ottawa Sun, 158

Parent Finders: aid with searches for adoptees and birth parents, 91–3, 96, 140, 163, 184; founding of, 85; Hamilton, 85; and legal cases, 88, 199–200, 212; lobbying for adoption disclosure reform, 10, 86, 88, 122–3, 140, 142, 147, 164, 178, 184, 199, 210; and Marilyn Churley, 91–3, 96, 110–11; Ottawa, 10, 85, 110–11, 147; protests, 122; Toronto, 10, 85, 122; Vancouver, 85, 122

Parsons, Ernie, 146–7, 148, 150

paternity, 82, 147, 150–1, 152, 174–6, 205, 212. *See also* biological fathers

Patton, Denbigh, 183

Perry (pseud., Marilyn Churley's first husband), 38–9, 48–51, 54, 55, 56, 59–66, 69–70, 202

Petrie, Anne, 113–14

Phillips, Gerry, 126

Philomena (film), 2

pollution. *See under* Churley, Marilyn, political

Pratten, Olivia, 215–16

pregnancy. *See* birth mothers: treatment of during pregnancy, birth, and adoption; Churley, Marilyn, personal; teen pregnancy; unmarried mothers

premarital sex, 1–2, 84, 113–14, 151–2. *See also* unmarried mothers

Prince Edward Island, abortion, 3

Prince Rupert, British Columbia, 74, 137

privacy. *See under* adoptees; adoption; adoption disclosure reform; contact veto; records, birth and adoption: disclosure veto

privacy commissioner. *See* Cavoukian, Ann

private member's bills. *See* individual bills

Progressive Conservative Party of Ontario (Ontario PC). *See also* individual members: amalgamation of Toronto, 105–8; deregulation and downloading, 142; government, 85–7, 93, 105–6, 127–8, 158–61, 164–5, 173; opposition to adoption disclosure reform, 11–12, 87, 126–8, 151–4, 158, 163, 178, 180, 186, 189,

190–2, 195, 196; support for adoption disclosure reform, 125–6, 156, 157–8, 196

promiscuity, 2–3, 34, 39, 84, 110, 113–14

protests and rallies at Queen's Park, 10, 106, 122, 141, *157*, 157–8

public hearings. *See under* adoption disclosure reform

Pupatello, Sandra, 167–8, 190–1, 192, 195–7

putative fathers. *See* biological fathers

Queen's Park. *See* protests and rallies at Queen's Park

Racco, Mario, 181

racism, 214–15. *See also* Aboriginal adoption

Radwanski, Adam, 192–3

Rae, Bob, 4, 9, 10, 80, 90, 93, 105, 173

Ramsay, David, 126

rape. *See* sexual assault

records, birth and adoption. *See also* adoption disclosure reform; contact veto: access for adoptees born outside the province, 212; access for adult adoptees, 5, 10–11, 83, 85–7, 89, 123, 125, 138, 139, 149, 166, 179, 182, 185, 199–200, 210; access for birth parents, 5, 89, 123, 124, 138, 139, 141, 166, 179, 185, 199–200, 210; access for extended family, 212; access in other jurisdictions, 125, 145, 167, 179, 180, 185, 209–10, 211, 212; adoption disclosure registry, 86–7, 89, 91, 95, 150, 163, 224; biological fathers, 147, 150, 211–12, 215; disclosure veto, 178, 179–80, 183–4, 198–200, 210, 211; and ethnicity, 10,

82; exemptions from disclosure, 186; government conducted searches, 89; and identity, 10, 82, 83, 125, 180, 194, 213–14, 218, 221; mandatory counselling, 89, 123; and medical history, 10, 82, 87, 89, 110, 119, 141, 145, 148, 155–6, 160, 172–3, 178, 180, 187, 189, 190, 211, 213, 218; non-identifying information, 86, 87, 89, 90, 95, 119, 179, 187, 213, 223–4; sealed, 10, 83, 140, 141, 200, 210; standards for time limits and veracity, 213

recycling, 77

Redmond, Wendie, 85

reform of adoption disclosure laws. *See* adoption disclosure reform

registrar general, 86, 89, 202, 212. *See also under* Churley, Marilyn, political

religion and church, 3, *17*, 30, 50–1, 90, 132, 141

Report of the Super of Neglected and Dependent Children, 84–5

reproductive rights, 3

reproductive technology, 215–18

residential schools, 213, 214

reunion of adoptees and birth parents: and counselling, 89, 123; as happy experience, 95, 113, 149, 177, 185, 188, 208; and healing, 5, 191–2; as negative experience, 126–7, 147, 148

Reville, David, 76, 80

Rice, Judy, 85

Richardson, Patricia, 85

right to privacy. *See under* adoption disclosure reform

rights of adoptees. *See under* adoptees

rights of birth mothers. *See under* birth mothers

PHOTOGRAPHY CREDIT

Photos pages i, 80, 101, and 240
courtesy of Marco Mancinelli.